Egypt and the Middle East
Ancient Times Through Modern Day

Author: Patrick Hotle, Ph.D.
Editors: Mary Dieterich and Sarah M. Anderson
Consultants: Schyrlet Cameron and Carolyn Craig
Proofreader: Margaret Brown

COPYRIGHT © 2012 Mark Twain Media, Inc.

ISBN 978-1-58037-625-9

Printing No. CD-404160

Mark Twain Media, Inc., Publishers
Distributed by Carson-Dellosa Publishing LLC

The purchase of this book entitles the buyer to reproduce the student pages for classroom use only. Other permissions may be obtained by writing Mark Twain Media, Inc., Publishers.

All rights reserved. Printed in the United States of America.

Visit us at www.carsondellosa.com

Table of Contents

Introduction to the Teacher	iii
National Standards Matrix	iv
Time Line for the Middle East	1
The Rise of Ancient Egypt	7
The Pyramids and the Sphinx	9
The Egyptian Gods	14
The End of the Old Kingdom	16
The Middle Kingdom	18
The End of the Middle Kingdom	21
The New Kingdom	23
Queen Hatshepsut	25
Akhenaton the Bizarre	27
The Tomb of Tutankhamen	29
The Rise and Fall of Empires in the Middle East	31
The Creative Nations of Phoenicia and Israel	33
Alexander the Great Conquers His World	35
The Middle East and the Roman Empire	37
Christianity Conquers Rome	39
From the Sands of Arabia Comes Islam	41
The Islamic Golden Age	43
Crusaders Descend Upon the Middle East	45
The Middle East Under the Power of the Turks	48
New Forces for Change in the Ottoman Empire	51
World War I and the Middle East	53
The Mandate System	56
The Middle East and World War II	59
Israel	62
Oil Brings Changes to the Middle East	65
Khomeini Takes on the United States	69
Saddam Hussein and Desert Storm	72
The PLO and Israel	75
The United States and the Middle East	78
Arab Spring	80
Glossary	83
Answer Keys	88
Bibliography	92
Photo Credits	C3

Introduction to the Teacher

Egypt and the Middle East is a valuable resource that can be used to supplement the social studies curriculum for middle-school students. It presents a broad tapestry of people and events and gives the student insight into historical events that have occurred in the Middle East. Each unit of study in the book is designed to strengthen history literacy skills and is correlated with National Curriculum Standards for Social Studies (NCSS). The book is part of the *Civilizations of the Past* series from Mark Twain Media, Inc.

The book is specifically designed to facilitate planning for the diverse learning styles and skill levels of middle-school students. The special features of the book provide the teacher with alternative methods of instruction. A modified version of the text is available for struggling readers.

Book Features
- **Reading Selection** introduces facts and information as a reading exercise.

- **Knowledge Check** assesses student understanding of the reading exercise using selected response and constructed response questioning strategies.

- **Map Follow-Up** provides opportunities for students to report information from a spatial perspective.

- **Explore** allows students to expand learning by participating in high-interest, hands-on activities.

- **Glossary** lists the boldfaced words with definitions.

Online Resources
Reluctant Reader Text: A modified version of the reading exercise pages can be downloaded from the website at www.carsondellosa.com. In the Search box, enter the product code CD-404160. When you reach the *Egypt and the Middle East* product page, click the icon for the Reluctant Reader Text download.

The readability level of the text has been modified to facilitate struggling readers. The Flesch-Kincaid Readability formula, which is build into Microsoft® Word™, was used to determine the readability level. The formula calculates the number of words, syllables, and sentences in each selection producing a reading level.

Additional Resources
Classroom Decoratives: *World Geography: Middle-East Maps* and *Ancient Civilizations and Cultures Topper* Bulletin Board Sets are available from Mark Twain Media/Carson-Dellosa Publishing LLC. These classroom decoratives visually reinforce lessons found in *Egypt and the Middle East* in an interesting and attention grabbing way.

National Standards Matrix

Units	Curriculum Standards for Social Studies									
	1	2	3	4	5	6	7	8	9	10
Time Line	x	x							x	
Maps	x	x	x	x	x	x				
The Rise of Ancient Egypt	x	x	x	x	x	x		x	x	
The Pyramids and the Sphinx	x	x	x	x	x	x	x	x	x	
The Egyptian Gods	x	x	x	x	x	x			x	
The End of the Old Kingdom	x	x	x	x	x	x	x	x	x	
The Middle Kingdom	x	x	x	x	x	x	x	x	x	
The End of the Middle Kingdom	x	x	x	x	x	x	x		x	
The New Kingdom	x	x	x	x	x	x			x	
Queen Hatshepsut	x	x	x	x	x	x	x		x	
Akhenaton the Bizarre	x	x	x	x	x	x			x	
The Tomb of Tutankhamen	x	x	x	x	x	x			x	
The Rise and Fall of Empires in the Middle East	x	x	x	x	x	x			x	
The Creative Nations of Phoenicia and Israel	x	x	x	x	x	x			x	
Alexander the Great Conquers His World	x	x	x	x	x	x			x	
The Middle East and the Roman Empire	x	x	x	x	x	x			x	
Christianity Conquers Rome	x	x	x	x	x	x	x		x	
From the Sands of Arabia Comes Islam	x	x	x	x	x	x			x	
The Islamic Golden Age	x	x	x	x	x	x	x	x	x	
Crusaders Descend Upon the Middle East	x	x	x	x	x	x	x	x	x	
The Middle East Under the Power of the Turks	x	x	x	x	x	x	x	x	x	
New Forces for Change in the Ottoman Empire	x	x	x	x	x	x		x	x	
World War I and the Middle East	x	x	x	x	x	x	x		x	
The Mandate System	x	x	x	x	x	x	x		x	
The Middle East and World War II	x	x	x	x	x	x	x		x	
Israel	x	x	x	x	x	x			x	
Oil Brings Changes to the Middle East	x	x	x	x	x	x	x	x	x	
Khomeini Takes on the United States	x	x	x	x	x	x	x	x	x	
Saddam Hussein and Desert Storm	x	x	x	x	x	x	x		x	
The PLO and Israel	x	x	x	x	x			x		
The United States and the Middle East	x	x	x	x	x	x			x	
Arab Spring	x	x	x	x	x	x			x	x

For more information on National Curriculum Standards for Social Studies, visit <http://www.ncss.org/standards>.

Time Line for the Middle East

The time line below provides facts and information about this time period. It shows when important events took place, in what order they occurred, and the amount of time that passed between them.

In the western world, we usually record years by reference to a year thought to be that of the birth of Jesus Christ or the year 1. The years before that are noted by how many years before that date they occurred. They are written with the abbreviation B.C. after the dates. Therefore, 500 B.C. came before 200 B.C. After the birth of Christ, we use the abbreviation A.D., which means *Anno Domini,* the Latin phrase for "the year of our Lord." However, instead of counting the years backward, as we do for B.C., we count the years forward up to the present year. In the very ancient past, it is impossible to know exact dates, so ca. is written before the date as an abbreviation of the Latin word *circa,* which means "around" or "about."

ca. 3000 B.C.	Narmer unites Egypt.
ca. 2686–2160 B.C.	The Egyptian Old Kingdom.
ca. 2600 B.C.	The Pyramid of Khufu is constructed.
ca. 2500 B.C.	Lugals or kings appear in Mesopotamia.
ca. 2334–2279 B.C.	Sargon is king of Akkad.
ca. 2040 B.C.	Nebhepetre Mentuhotep reunifies Egypt.
ca. 2040–1633 B.C.	The Egyptian Middle Kingdom.
ca. 2000 B.C.	The Epic of Gilgamesh is written.
ca. 1800–1600 B.C.	Phoenicians develop alphabet.
ca. 1800 B.C.	Hyksos invasion of Egypt begins.
ca. 1800 B.C.	Abraham leads people out of Ur.
ca. 1792–1750 B.C.	Hammurabi is king of Babylonia.
ca. 1558–1085 B.C.	The Egyptian New Kingdom.
ca. 1558–1533 B.C.	Pharaoh Amosis I drives out the Hyksos.
ca. 1512–1500 B.C.	Thutmose I rules Egypt.
ca. 1490–1469 B.C.	Queen Hatshepsut rules Egypt.
ca. 1490–1436 B.C.	Thutmose III rules Egypt.
ca. 1450–1200 B.C.	Hittite empire thrives.
ca. 1353–1336 B.C.	Amenhotep IV (Akhenaton) rules Egypt, also known as the Amarna period.
ca. 1334–1325 B.C.	Tutankhamen rules Egypt.
ca. 1300 B.C.	Moses leads Hebrews out of Egypt.
ca. 1300–1287 B.C.	Pharaoh Seti I wins back lost lands.
ca. 1286 B.C.	The battle of Kadesh.
ca. 1270–1220 B.C.	Ramses II, ruler of Egypt, builds Karnak.
ca. 1198–1166 B.C.	Pharaoh Ramses III resists invasion of Sea Peoples.
ca. 1000–961 B.C.	David is king of Israel.
ca. 961–922 B.C.	Solomon oversees golden age of Israel.
ca. 922 B.C.	Judah breaks off from Israel.
ca. 722 B.C.	Assyrians destroy Israel.
ca. 700–500 B.C.	Assyrian Empire thrives.

The Narmer Pallette from ca. 3100 B.C. shows the pharaoh smiting the enemies of Egypt.

ca. 586 B.C.	Chaldeans destroy Jerusalem and begin the Babylonian captivity.
ca. 571 B.C.	Phoenician city of Tyre falls to Chaldeans.
ca. 550 B.C.	Cyrus the Great establishes the Persian Empire.
ca. 550–350 B.C.	Persian Empire thrives.
460–430 B.C.	The golden age of Athens.
338 B.C.	Philip II of Macedon defeats Athens.
336–323 B.C.	Reign of Alexander the Great.
264 B.C.	Rome controls all of Italy.
31 B.C.	Battle of Actium.
ca. 4 B.C.	Jesus Christ born.
29 B.C. to A.D. 14	Most of the Middle East falls under Roman control.
A.D. 10–200	Pax Romana.
A.D. 70	Jerusalem destroyed by Titus and beginning of the Diaspora.
A.D. 284–305	Diocletian is emperor of Rome and the empire is divided.
312	Emperor Constantine issues Edict of Milan, granting toleration to Christians.
330	Constantinople is constructed and beginning of Byzantine civilization.
610	Muhammad called upon to begin Islam.
632	Islam begins to spread to Middle East.
640	Persia comes under Muslim rule.
711	Muslim invasion of Spain.
738	Arab merchant colony in Canton, China.
762	Abbasid Caliph al-Mansur moves capital to Baghdad.
813	The mathematician Chwarazmi thrives in Baghdad; coins the term *algebra*.
925	The Arab physician al-Razi dies.
1055	Seljuk Turks seize Baghdad.
1099	First Crusade captures Jerusalem.
1154	Muhammad al-Idrisi finishes circular map of the world.
1187	Saladin recaptures Jerusalem from Crusaders.
1204	Fourth Crusade captures Constantinople from Byzantine emperor.
1258	Mongols capture Baghdad and end the Caliphate.
1353	Alhambra completed in Granada, Spain.
1453	Constantinople falls to the Ottomans and ends the Roman Empire in the East.
1492	Last Muslim stronghold in Spain (Granada) falls to Ferdinand and Isabella.

The Alhambra was a palace and fortress built by the Moors on a hill overlooking the city of Granada, Spain.

1498	Portuguese explorer Vasco de Gama sails to India via the Cape of Good Hope.
1520	Suleiman the Magnificent begins his 46-year reign.
1529	Ottoman siege of Vienna fails.
1699	Ottoman Empire begins to lose territory in Europe.
1774	Ottomans lose territory to the Russians at the treaty of Kuchuk Kainarji.
1798	Napoleon invades Egypt.
1805	Muhammad Ali becomes ruler of Egypt.
1828	First Arab language newspaper established in Egypt.
1829	Greece wins independence from Ottomans.
1839	The Tanzimat era of reform begins in the Ottoman Empire.
1853–1856	Crimean War.
1869	Suez Canal opened.
1897	First Zionist congress in Basel, Switzerland.
1898	Ottomans persuaded to extend railroad to Baghdad by German Kaiser.
1907	Britain and France agree to divide domination of Persia between them.
1908	Young Turks seize control of the Ottoman Empire.
1914	Assassination of Archduke Franz Ferdinand begins World War I.
1915	Gallipoli landing fails to capture Dardanelles; Lawrence of Arabia operating against Turks.
1917	United States enters the war. Wilson announces Fourteen Points. The British cabinet approves the Balfour Declaration.
1918	Ottoman Empire surrenders. World War I ends.
1918–1920	Mandate system established.
1922	Ataturk deposes last Ottoman sultan; proclaims Turkey a republic.
1925	French crush rebellion in Damascus and Reza Khan comes to power in Iran.
1930	Syria writes a constitution but remains under French control.
1931	Iraq granted independence.
1936	British troops leave Cairo but occupy the Suez Canal; Palestinian Arabs riot.
1937	Peel Commission sent to Palestine.
1939	World War II begins; British White Paper denies policy of creating Jewish state.
1941	Lebanon granted independence. Rashid Ali becomes premier of Iraq; Mohammad Reza Pahlavi becomes Shah of Iran.
1942	Battle of El Alamein.
1945	Syria granted independence.
1946	Transjordan granted independence.
1948	Jewish state of Israel created; war between Israel and Arab States.
1949	Ben-Gurion becomes prime minister of Israel.
1951	Iranian Premier Mossadegh nationalizes Anglo-Iranian Oil Company.
1953	Hussein becomes king of Jordan; U.S.–aided coup overthrows Mossadegh.
1954	Nasser comes to power in Egypt.
1956	Suez Canal Crisis.
1958	United Arab Republic formed; Iraqi coup kills king.

1960	OPEC formed.
1961	Kuwait granted independence.
1964	Ayatollah Khomeini exiled from Iran; foundation of Palestine Liberation Organization (PLO).
1967	Six-Day War.
1968	Charter of the PLO drafted.
1969	PLO chooses Arafat as leader.
1970	PLO expelled from Jordan.
1973	Yom Kippur War; OPEC raises price of oil 400 percent.
1977	Kuwait nationalizes oil wells; Egyptian President Anwar Sadat visits Israel.
1978	U.S.-brokered peace between Israel and Egypt. Shah Mohammad Reza Pahlavi imposes martial rule in Iran.
1979	Egypt expelled from Arab League. Radical Muslims seize Grand Mosque in Mecca; failed coup attempt in Saudi Arabia; Iranian revolution, led by Khomeini, expels shah from Iran; U.S. hostages taken; Saddam Hussein becomes President of Iraq; Egyptian-Israeli treaty signed by Sadat and Israel's Prime Minister, Menachem Begin, at Camp David in the United States.
1980	Iran-Iraq War begins; U.S. attempt to free hostages in Iran fails.
1981	U.S. hostages held by Iranian militants are released.
1985	Egypt re-admitted to Arab League.
1987	Intifada begins and Iraqi missiles hit U.S. destroyer.
1988	Iran-Iraq War ends.
1990	Iraq invades Kuwait.
1991	Operation Desert Shield/Desert Storm launched against Iraq.
1992	Madrid Peace Conference creates plan for Palestinian self-rule.
1993	Oslo Accords: PLO recognizes Israel's right to exist in peace; Israel recognizes the PLO as the representative of the Palestinian people.
2001	Islamic terrorists attack the United States; United States, Great Britain, and Afghan United Front launch Operation Enduring Freedom, the official name of the war in Afghanistan.
2003	United States declares war on Iraq as part of the War on Terror.
2011	Osama bin Laden, founder of al-Qaeda, killed by Special Forces of the United States; President Obama started troop withdraw from Afghanistan and announced withdrawal of forces from Iraq; Arab Spring, a democratic uprising started in one Arab country and then rapidly spread across the Middle East.

Egypt and the Middle East Time Line for the Middle East

Name: _____ Date: _____

Knowledge Check

Order of Events
Number the events in order from 1 (first) to 10 (last). Use the time line for reference.

_____ A. Arab Spring, a democratic uprising, spread across the Middle East.
_____ B. A group called the Young Turks seize control of the Ottoman Empire.
_____ C. The Pax Romana was a long period of peace experienced by the Roman Empire.
_____ D. The United States launches Operation Enduring Freedom.
_____ E. The Suez Canal is opened.
_____ F. The Islamic religion begins to spread through the Middle East.
_____ G. The First Crusade captures Jerusalem.
_____ H. The Jewish state of Israel is created.
_____ I. The Phoenicians develop an alphabet.
_____ J. The Persian Empire is established by Cyrus the Great.

True or False
Circle *T* for True or *F* for False

1. T F   Operation Desert Storm was launched against Iran.
2. T F   The Babylonian captivity began with the Chaldeans destroying Jerusalem.
3. T F   The first Arab language newspaper was established in Egypt.
4. T F   The Six-Day War was in 1967.
5. T F   Around 1200 B.C., Moses led the Hebrews out of Egypt.

Constructed Response
6. Time lines are efficient graphic organizers that provide a tool for studying events in history. Explain how a time line can be helpful using details from the Time Line for the Middle East to support your answer.

_____
_____
_____
_____
_____
_____
_____

Egypt and the Middle East | Time Line for the Middle East

Name: _____ Date: _____

Explore: String Time Line

Materials
Time Line of Middle East pages   5" x 8" blank index cards   yarn
tape   markers   colored pencils

Directions: Create a time line.

Step 1: Research 10 events from the Time Line of the Middle East pages.

Step 2: Record the information for each event on a different index card. At the top of the card, glue magazine pictures or computer-generated graphics, or sketch a picture to illustrate the event. Below the illustration, write the date the event occurred. At the bottom of the card, write a brief description of the event.

Step 3: On a table, organize the cards in chronological order from earliest to latest date.

Step 4: Cut a piece of yarn 2 meters long. Tape the cards to the string. Leave enough string on both ends to allow the time line to be tied, taped, or tacked up on display.

Date: Ruled ca. 1334–1325 B.C.

Description: Tutankhamen was crowned king of Egypt when he was ten years old. As king, he had the temples to the god Aton dismantled and used the materials to build new temples to the god Amon-Re. He was buried, like the rest of the New Kingdom pharaohs, in the Valley of the Kings.

The Rise of Ancient Egypt

By 2700 B.C., the people who lived along the Nile River had created a sophisticated and vibrant **civilization** that lasted for thousands of years. These ancient Egyptians built huge stone **monuments** and **temples**. They also created a system of writing.

Historians have divided Egyptian history into three distinct **eras**: the **Old Kingdom** (2686–2160 B.C.), the **Middle Kingdom** (2040–1633 B.C.), and the **New Kingdom** (1558–1085 B.C.). The eras are divided by years during which the central government broke down. These spaces between the kingdoms are known as **Intermediate Periods**.

The Nile River

Egypt has been described as "the gift of the Nile." Egyptian civilization was shaped by its close proximity to a river. Egypt was dry and relied on irrigation to collect and distribute water. The Nile River served as an avenue for transport to Egyptian cities. Here food, fuel, and the building materials that were used to construct the **pyramids** could be transported. Water from the Nile could also be channeled to arid lands away from the river all year long. Almost all Egyptians lived in the narrow belt and fan-shaped **delta** of fertile land shaped by the Nile.

The **Nile River** runs from south to north. The Egyptians called the land in the south **Upper Egypt**, while the delta region in the north they called **Lower Egypt**. Its annual floods were not only predictable, but were looked forward to by the Egyptians. The floods brought water and fresh, black soil from upriver to **rejuvenate** the land. As a result, Egyptian agriculture was the most successful of the ancient world.

This small statue represented the spirit of the Nile River in flood, which brought the Egyptians fertile soil.

The Nile River is protected on the east and west by deserts too vast for most invaders to cross. Thus, Egypt developed a **homogeneous** civilization of its own, developing without much outside interference. In Egypt, there was plenty of water and rich farm land. Because of these advantages, the Egyptians were an **optimistic** people. For instance, they believed in an **afterlife** as good as, if not better than, the present. Each year the Nile brought new life to Egyptian agriculture, so they believed death must only be a brief season before an afterlife in the next world.

Historians also believe that faith in the unchanging nature of life helped to promote the idea of a single, all-powerful king. He was known as the **pharaoh**. This ruler supplied Egyptians with a strong central government, an elaborate bureaucracy to manage the complex irrigation system, and a living symbol of order to worship. The stability of life also gives Egyptian history remarkable continuity. Religion, fashion, language, art, and social tradition remained basically unchanged. A day in the life of an Egyptian changed little during the 3,000 years we call ancient Egypt.

An Egyptian Woman and Man

Knowledge Check

Matching

___ 1. civilization
___ 2. afterlife
___ 3. era
___ 4. pharaoh
___ 5. rejuvenate
___ 6. delta
___ 7. pyramids

a. a certain time period in history
b. the flat, fan-shaped land made of silt deposited at the mouth of a river
c. to restore
d. the life after death
e. the title used by the rulers of ancient Egypt
f. the massive structures built of stone, usually having a square base and four triangular sides that slope upward
g. a culture that has developed systems of religion, learning, and government

Multiple Choice

8. Which way does the Nile River run?
   a. from north to south
   b. from south to north
   c. from east to west
   d. from west to east

9. What was the delta region in the north called?
   a. Lower Egypt
   b. Upper Egypt
   c. Lower Africa
   d. Upper Africa

10. What protected the Nile River on the east and west from invaders?
    a. Egyptian warriors
    b. infested swamps
    c. vast deserts
    d. giant pyramids

Constructed Response

11. Explain why Egypt has been described as "the gift of the Nile." Use two details from the selection to support your answer.

___
___
___
___
___
___

The Pyramids and the Spinx

Ask the average person today to name three things about ancient Egypt, and they will probably answer "pyramids, the Sphinx, and mummies." If asked why the Egyptians erected the colossal pyramids and the Sphinx and mummified the bodies of the dead, they might give a good answer. But if asked how it was done, they will be stumped because we can only guess about their methods.

Mummies

The Egyptians were strong believers in life after death. They believed a complete body was needed to house the soul, or **ka**, so they developed a process to keep the body preserved. The bodies of the wealthier Egyptians were taken to the City of the Dead, where those trained in the procedure turned the body into a **mummy**. Those who knew the secret were not going to reveal their methods in writing because they did not want competition. The procedure was rather gruesome, and we have a good idea of how it was done, but the chemicals used to preserve the mummy remain a mystery. Most likely it was a salt called natron that dried out the bodies. We know it was a long process because the time between death and burial was 70 days.

The Sphinx

The great **Sphinx** sits proudly near the pyramid of the pharaoh Khafre and was built with blocks of stone remaining after that pyramid was completed. The lion body is 240 feet long, and the human head wearing the royal headpiece rises 66 feet above the base. It is certain that the features of the face are those of Khafre and that the Sphinx was built to honor him. Later, pharaohs used the Sphinx as a symbol of their god-given right to rule. The Sphinx today suffers from abuse by man and desert sandstorms, but considering that it was built between c.a. 2575 and 2467 B.C., it reflects well on its builders.

The Pyramids of Egypt

The most massive projects of the Middle Eastern world were the pyramids. They were built to honor a pharaoh and provide him with a tomb worthy of his glory. Work on the pyramid began while the pharaoh was alive and continued many years after his death. Around the bases of the pyramids, large palaces, temples, and storerooms were built. Here priests would oversee the worship of the pharaoh's spirit long after he was dead. Outside the temple complex, much smaller pyramids for the queens were constructed, and beyond those were flat tombs called **mastabas** for the pharaoh's officials. In the Old Kingdom, an afterlife was reserved for only the pharaoh and his officials. The pharaoh was perceived as a god. He was considered the child of the Sun god Re. This god-king ruled over his realm according to the principle of **ma'at**, which meant order, justice, and truth.

The 80 pyramids of Egypt were located west of the Nile River and in the desert beyond irrigated land. Most of the large pyramids were built between the third and sixth dynasties, in the period of the Old Kingdom, all within 20 miles of the ancient capital of Memphis at a place called Gizeh. Herodotus, the Greek historian, estimated that 100,000 men worked for 20 years in the seasons between Nile floods to complete the Great Pyramid.

Pyramid Construction

The base of each pyramid was the same. All were square at the base. The so-called **Great Pyramid** built in honor of Khufu (Cheops) had a base 755 feet long and stood 481 feet tall. Construction was so precise that the measurements at the base were correct within six-tenths of an inch. The angles of the sides make an almost perfect triangle.

The Great Pyramid Built for Khufu

Construction involved some very difficult geometric calculations, all made without the aid of a computer. Consider the problems. Everything had to be built perfectly level, otherwise it would never look right. Using water in trenches to test levels, Egyptians were so accurate in building the Great Pyramid that the northwest corner stands only a half inch lower than the southeast corner. Then they had to find the rock to cut and move it from the **quarry** 600 miles away to the building site. Once there, groups of 18 to 20 men pulled the two-and-a-half-ton stone block up a ramp until it reached its proper spot on the pyramid.

Since the purpose was to create a place for the pharaoh's body to lie in splendor, a burial chamber was built deep inside the pyramid. Included there were the **Pyramid Texts**, instructions to the pharaoh on how to guide his vessel through the underworld to the sky to Re, the Sun god. A passageway was constructed so the workers assigned to prepare the chamber could climb to the tomb. After their work was done, it was their route for leaving. To keep grave robbers out, stones were dropped in place when the workers left. These passageways created the threat of internal collapse that might bring down the whole structure. This required heavy granite slabs to be laid over the king's chamber.

Not all pyramids looked exactly alike. The first one attempted was built for King Djoser and was designed by his brilliant architect, Imhotep. It was called the **stepped pyramid** because its sides resemble six steps climbing to the top. The pyramid of King Snefru is called the **bent pyramid** because the angle was steeper at the base than in the top half. The later pyramids also differed in size and the types of stone used.

The monuments of Egypt stand today as testimony to Egypt's religion, knowledge of mathematics, skill in building huge structures, and the glory of the pharaohs.

The stepped pyramid (left) was built for King Djoser, and the bent pyramid (right) was built for King Snefru.

Egypt and the Middle East

The Pyramids and the Sphinx

Name: _____ Date: _____

Knowledge Check

Matching

_____ 1. ka
_____ 2. Sphinx
_____ 3. mastabas
_____ 4. ma'at
_____ 5. Great Pyramid
_____ 6. Pyramid Texts
_____ 7. stepped pyramid
_____ 8. bent pyramid

a. a ruling principle of the pharoah meaning order, justice, and truth
b. a large stone sculpture with a lion body and human head
c. a pyramid whose sides resemble steps
d. flat tombs for the pharoah's officials
e. a pyramid whose base is steeper than its top half
f. the term the Egyptians used for the soul
g. largest pyramid at Gizeh
h. instructions to the pharoah on how to guide his vessel through the underworld to the Sun god

Multiple Choice

9. Who was the great Sphinx built to honor?
   a. Snefru
   b. Khufu
   c. Djoser
   d. Khafre

10. The time between death and burial in which the body was turned into a mummy was how long?
    a. 6 weeks
    b. 70 days
    c. 120 days
    d. 6 months

11. To test that the pyramid was being built on a level surface, trenches were filled with what?
    a. water
    b. oil
    c. rocks
    d. mud

Constructed Response

12. How would the Egyptians have felt about cremation? Use details from the reading selection to support your answer.

_____
_____
_____
_____
_____

Map Follow-Up: Egypt

Directions: Using the map below and an atlas or the Internet, match the names of the modern nations and physical features listed below with the numbers on the map.

___ Saudi Arabia ___ Egypt ___ Jordan ___ Israel
___ Sudan ___ Red Sea ___ Sinai Peninsula ___ Nile River
___ Mediterranean Sea ___ Gulf of Suez

Using the map below and an atlas or the Internet, locate and label the modern cities of Alexandria, Aswan, Asyut, Cairo, and Suez. Also locate and label Gizeh (Giza), which is just south of modern-day Cairo on the west side of the river.

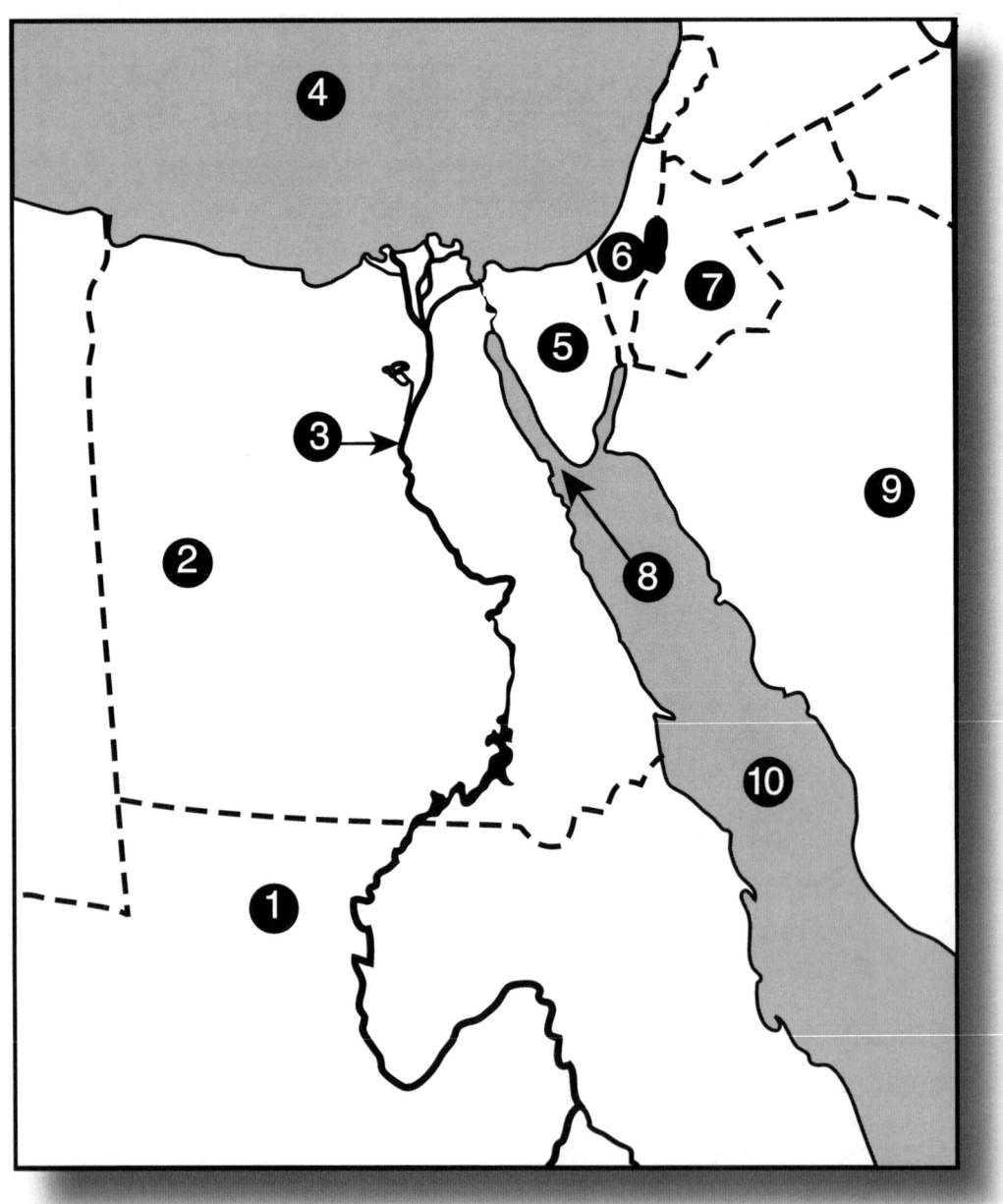

Explore: Egyptian Numerals

The Egyptian number system used seven different hieroglyphic symbols. Egyptian engineers and mathematicians used the number symbols to build the pyramids in the Nile Valley.

NUMBER	SIGN
1	│
10	∩
100	℗
1,000	𓆼

NUMBER	SIGN
10,000	𓂭
100,000	𓆐
1,000,000	𓁨

The number 142 would be written in the Egyptian number system like this:

100 + 40 + 2 = ℗ ∩∩ ∩∩ ││

Directions: Try reading and writing numbers using the Egyptian number system.

1. What is the value of each Egyptian number written below?

   a. _____

   b. _____

   c. _____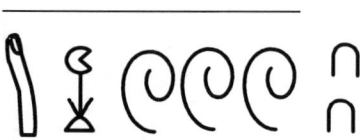

   d. _____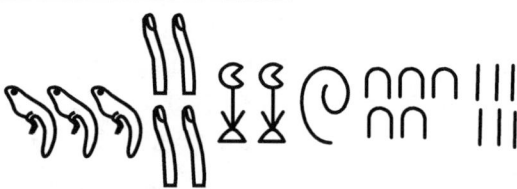

2. In the space below, write the number 1,342,154 using the Egyptian number system.

The Egyptian Gods

Egyptian Religion

The religion of the ancient Egyptians was a mixture of many beliefs. Egyptian **mythology** taught that the sky was a goddess named **Nut** who stretched over the earth. At other times, it was believed the sky was a very large cow. Six different gods represented the moon. Mixing conflicting beliefs is called **syncretism**. This did not bother the Egyptians. To them, these different beliefs were all valid ways of describing nature.

A Land of Many Gods

The Sun God Ra

Horus, the God of Light

Egyptian gods took many forms. From earliest times the most important god was **Re**, or **Ra**. He was the god of the Sun. Re was worshipped by all Egyptians. Other gods were worshipped only in certain cities or regions. In the Old Kingdom, he became the official god of the nation. However, the Egyptians worshipped over 2,000 different gods. The most common forms were animals. **Horus** was portrayed as a falcon. **Anubis** was the judge of the dead. He had the head of a jackal. Other gods combined parts of many animals. **Tawert** was the goddess of childbirth. Her body was made up of the body parts of a hippopotamus, crocodile, and lioness. Live animals associated with gods were often kept and worshipped. For example, crocodiles represented the god **Sobek**. They were worshipped and lived a life of luxury in the temple pool of Crocodilopolis. When they died, they were made into mummies. They were placed in tombs like humans.

Sometimes the Egyptians turned real people into gods. The **pharaohs** were worshipped while still alive. A few pharaohs or great men were so well-liked that they were worshipped after they died. For example, the builder of the very first pyramid, **Imhotep**, was considered a god of wisdom.

Worshipping

Most ancient Egyptians had only limited access to **temples**. These were places where the gods were worshipped. They might only see the statues at festival time. The priests would bring out the images and carry them around the city on their shoulders. However, the Egyptian people could always express their devotion to a god or goddess by owning small **amulets** or statuettes. Sometimes furniture was decorated with the face of a god or goddess. For example, the image of **Bes**, one of the gods of the family, was placed on eating utensils or children's cradles. Also, there were parts of the temples set aside for people who wanted to make special appeals to the gods. Sometimes, gods were called upon to grant special requests. Water poured over the image of **Hor-pa-khered** was believed to have special power to cure poisonous bites and stings.

Sobek was the god of the Nile. Crocodiles were so feared, they were worshipped as gods.

Egypt and the Middle East

The Egyptian Gods

Name: _____ Date: _____

Knowledge Check

Matching

_____ 1. pharaoh   a. a building devoted to the worship of a god or gods

_____ 2. mythology   b. the tendency to combine contradictory beliefs

_____ 3. Anubis   c. the judge of the dead

_____ 4. amulets   d. the title used by the rulers of ancient Egypt

_____ 5. Tawert   e. a traditional story accepted as history

_____ 6. syncretism   f. a goddess of childbirth

_____ 7. temple   g. a small ornament or piece of jewelry

Multiple Choice

8. Who was the most important god to the Egyptians?
   a. Re
   b. Horus
   c. Tawert
   d. Hathor

9. Who was considered a god of wisdom?
   a. Re
   b. Tawert
   c. Sobek
   d. Imhotep

10. Who was one of the gods of the family?
    a. Sobek
    b. Imhotep
    c. Bes
    d. Horus

Constructed Response

11. Using information from the selection, give some examples of how the religion of the ancient Egyptians was complex.

_____

_____

_____

_____

_____

_____

_____

_____

The End of the Old Kingdom

Pepi II Shown With His Mother

Fall of the Old Kingdom

The Old Kingdom came to an end with the reign of Pepi II. He was eight years old when be became pharaoh, and he ruled for the next 90 years. Pepi II was never a brilliant ruler, and he probably lost interest in the job by the time of his old age. At that time, rulers were supposed to be above worry, so the old pharaoh left details of state to be handled by others, giving influence and power to those who ruled in the name of the pharaoh. When Pepi II died, so did centralized power. Egypt entered an era of rulers who were called pharaohs, but commanded no respect. One did not need to be a member of the pharaoh's family to become a high official anymore. The short **reigns** of these pharaohs indicate that the situation was unstable. One pharaoh was quickly overthrown by another.

Historians and **archaeologists** are uncertain why the Old Kingdom fell. One possible explanation offered is the cost of constructing so many pyramids. Pharaohs borrowed money from nobles in return for land or special privileges. In time, the **provincial** governors, called **nomarchs**, became so powerful that their offices became **hereditary**, and they could challenge the pharaoh's power. As the pharaoh's power declined, there was no one to administer justice or manage irrigation. At the same time, the **monsoon rains** in Ethiopia, which filled the Nile River with water, slackened. As a result, Egypt was swept with drought and famine. In addition to ransacked **tombs**, the surviving sources from the period paint a picture of **anarchy** with brother fighting brother, cannibalism, government files thrown into the streets, and Egypt divided between two opposing kingdoms. This is the **First Intermediate Period**. It came to an end when the country was at last **reunified** under Pharaoh Nebhepetre Mentuhotep in 2040 B.C.

A Stela From the First Intermediate Period

The Middle Kingdom

The strain of the First Intermediate Period had a profound effect on the Egyptians. As a result, many things changed. The new pharaohs abandoned the old capital of Memphis for a new one further south called Thebes. They began to make their sons co-rulers so that they could gain experience ruling and be sure that no one would challenge their right to rule when the old pharaoh died. They were determined to avoid the anarchy of the First Intermediate Period.

The attitude toward the pharaoh changed. No longer was he the remote **god-king** of the Old Kingdom. Instead, the pharaoh now appeared more like the good shepherd of his people. In the Middle Kingdom, the more realistic statues show rulers with concerned and even worried looks on their faces. These portraits reflect the general mood of the times. The writings from the Middle Kingdom show an inward-looking and serious Egyptian **society** interested in a sense of common **humanity** and **ethics**.

Egypt and the Middle East — The End of the Old Kingdom

Name: _____ Date: _____

Knowledge Check

Matching

_____ 1. tombs
_____ 2. reign
_____ 3. ethics
_____ 4. anarchy
_____ 5. reunified
_____ 6. archaeologist
_____ 7. society

a. a state of disorder due to the absence of authority
b. to bring a country back together after being divided
c. a set of moral ideas that rule a group's behavior
d. the large vaults, typically underground, used for burying the dead
e. a community of people living in a particular region and sharing customs, laws, and organizations
f. the rule of a king or queen
g. a person who studies the remains of past cultures

Multiple Choice

8. How long did Pepi II reign?
   a. 70 years
   b. 80 years
   c. 90 years
   d. 20 years

9. What was the name of the new capital in the Middle Kingdom?
   a. Memphis
   b. Thebes
   c. Ethiopia
   d. Springfield

10. In the Middle Kingdom, the pharaoh became more like a
    a. cruel tyrant.
    b. god-king.
    c. weak puppet.
    d. good shepherd.

A Pharaoh of the Middle Kingdom

Constructed Response

11. Explain possible causes for the First Intermediate Period. Use at least two details from the selection to support your answer.

_____
_____
_____
_____
_____
_____

The Middle Kingdom

The Afterlife Opens to Ordinary People

The period of the Middle Kingdom brought new interest in **ethics**, or right and wrong. This meant that the afterlife became open to other people besides the pharaoh. Even ordinary Egyptians, if they could afford to buy the right inscriptions of funeral prayers and spells, could be assured of an **eternal** life. This was made easier by the existence of paper, or **papyrus**. This came from weaving fibers from the papyrus plant that grew in abundance along the Nile.

Model of an Egyptian House Made of Pottery and Used in a Burial

Hieroglyphic Writing

On the papyrus, the Egyptians used **hieroglyphic** writing to record these prayers and spells. Hieroglyphic writing was done by drawing pictures. Before the Old Kingdom, when Egyptians first began to use hieroglyphics, the pictures were probably supposed to mean what they represented. For example, a picture of a basket meant a basket. As time went by, however, they found this too limiting and complicated. The Egyptians found that they could be more precise if they used pictures to represent sounds. Then it would be possible to spell out things that would be difficult to convey by pictures.

There were 600 different hieroglyphics representing the sounds found in the spoken Egyptian language. These hieroglyphics were used the same way we use the letters of the alphabet. Some hieroglyphs, however, continued to mean what their pictures represented. The hieroglyph showing an ox meant just that.

The Egyptian **scribes** were professional writers. They also had another method of writing called **hieratic**. This was a shorthand form in cursive for administration, accounting, and legal documents. As a result of contacts between Egypt and Greece, it finally evolved into a language known as **Coptic**.

Most Egyptians couldn't read or write hieroglyphics. Reading and writing were skills learned only by the scribes. Like other occupations in ancient Egypt such as farming or carpentry, the knowledge of the scribe was passed along from father to son. Many of the scribes worked in the pharaoh's government and became powerful men.

In their tombs, Egyptians buried with them all that they believed they would need in the next life. Archaeologists have not only found papyrus scrolls containing prayers and spells but also historical records, poetry, technical reports on mathematics and medicine, wisdom stories, letters between government officials, business contracts, and royal proclamations. It is largely because of the survival of these papyrus records that we know so much about Egyptian life during that time.

Most of the great works of Egyptian literature were written during the Middle Kingdom. The society that they describe was peaceful, balanced, and refined.

An Egyptian Scribe

Knowledge Check

Matching

_____ 1. papyrus
_____ 2. scribe
_____ 3. hieratic
_____ 4. ethics
_____ 5. hieroglyphic
_____ 6. eternal
_____ 7. Coptic

a. a professional writer who kept records and copied letters and official documents
b. a shorthand cursive form of ancient Egyptian writing; simpler than hieroglyphics
c. to exist forever
d. the ancient Egyptian system of writing that used symbols to stand for objects, ideas, or sounds
e. language that developed as a result of contacts between Egypt and Greece
f. a set of moral ideas that rule a group's behavior
g. a kind of paper made from a plant growing along the Nile River

Multiple Choice

8. How many kinds of hieroglyphs are found in the Egyptian language?
   a. 400   b. 500   c. 800   d. 600

9. Who did all of the reading and writing in ancient Egypt?
   a. carpenters
   b. scribes
   c. pharaohs
   d. basket weavers

10. How are hieroglyphics created?
    a. by drawing pictures
    b. by drawing letters
    c. by drawing sounds
    d. by drawing ideas

Khonsu Temple at Karnak

Constructed Response

11. Explain why we know so much about Egyptian life. Use details from the selection to support your answer.

_____
_____
_____
_____
_____
_____

Egypt and the Middle East — The Middle Kingdom

Name: _____ Date: _____

Explore: Hieroglyph Writing

The writing called hieroglyphics was used by the ancient Egyptians for 4,000 years. It used pictures to represent different objects, actions, sounds, or ideas. There were more than 600 hieroglyphs.

Directions: A cartouche (kar-toosh) is an oval-like shape that surrounds the hieroglyphs that make up the name of an Egyptian god or royal person. Use hieroglyphs to write your name in the cartouche below.

The End of the Middle Kingdom

Improving Egyptian Life

The Egyptians of the Middle Kingdom were travelers and traders. They traveled to the Punt region on the east coast of Africa to get **frankincense** and **myrrh**, which were necessary to Egyptian religious ceremonies. Traders also traveled to Nubia in the south to bring back gold. In the northeast, Egyptian ships sailed to Byblos on the coast of Lebanon to bring back cedar logs. From the island of Crete across the Mediterranean came olive oil. **Imported** products were necessary for many aspects of Egyptian life.

The Middle Kingdom pharaohs were interested not only in improving Egyptian life through foreign trade, but they also hoped to avoid some of the problems that had led to the collapse of the Old Kingdom. The powerful **provincial** governors who had defied the Old Kingdom pharaohs were weakened. Also, a gigantic irrigation project moved water from the Nile to a natural **depression** called Lake Faiyum where it could be stored for use during the dry season.

The Hyksos

The Middle Kingdom, however, was severely weakened by excessive flooding of the Nile. At the same time, the ruling family of the pharaohs died out. As a result, the question of who was to sit on the throne became a source of conflict between provincial governors. Egypt again split into two kingdoms, each trying to dominate the other. Egypt was left weakened as it faced a new danger from beyond its borders, the **Hyksos**.

Chariots helped the Hyksos defeat the Egyptians.

Around 1800 B.C. these mysterious invaders began to sweep across the border into Egypt from Syria and Palestine. The Egyptian armies were no match for them. The **invaders** brought new weapons that enabled them to easily defeat the Egyptians. Most terrifying of all, the Hyksos rode in a war machine not seen before in Egypt, the horse-drawn **chariot**.

These sphinxes represent Hyksos pharaohs.

After burning cities and destroying temples, the Hyksos leaders established themselves as pharaohs. Thus began the period in Egyptian history known as the **Second Intermediate Period** (1674–1558 B.C.).

An Egyptian pharaoh still ruled in Upper Egypt but was under the control of the Hyksos pharaoh in Lower Egypt. The Hyksos pharaohs ruled wisely. Instead of imposing their own ways, they adapted and borrowed from the Egyptians. Much of the administration remained in Egyptian hands. Hyksos kings also built temples to Egyptian gods, adopted Egyptian hieroglyphics, and copied Middle Kingdom styles of sculpture.

At first the Egyptians and Hyksos lived together without difficulty. Eventually, however, the Egyptian pharaoh in Upper Egypt grew strong enough to challenge the invaders for control of Egypt. They soon discovered that the Hyksos would not leave without a fight.

Egypt and the Middle East — The End of the Middle Kingdom

Name: _____ Date: _____

Knowledge Check

Matching

_____ 1. chariot
_____ 2. invaders
_____ 3. frankincense
_____ 4. imported
_____ 5. provincial
_____ 6. depression

a. a fragrant gum resin obtained from an African tree and burned as incense
b. brought into a country from somewhere else
c. a group of people who enter by force in order to conquer
d. a light, two-wheeled, horse-drawn vehicle used in ancient warfare and racing
e. to come from a province of a country or empire
f. a low, sunken hole

Multiple Choice

7. What was the most terrifying of all of the new weapons that the invaders used against the Egyptians?
   a. bow and arrows
   b. cannon
   c. catapult
   d. horse-drawn chariot

8. Around 1800 B.C., this tribe invaded Egypt from Syria and Palestine.
   a. Hyksos
   b. Syrians
   c. Provincial governors
   d. Nubians

9. How did the Egyptians use Lake Faiyum?
   a. as a place to swim
   b. as a place to store water
   c. as a place to bathe
   d. as a place to worship

Constructed Response

10. Explain how the Middle Kingdom hoped to avoid the problems that brought down the Old Kingdom. Use details from the selection to support your answer.

_____
_____
_____
_____
_____
_____
_____

The New Kingdom

Around 1500 B.C., Pharaoh Amosis defeated and **expelled** the Hyksos. For the first time in Egyptian history, the pharaoh had a professional standing army. A career in the army became a way for men of talent to move up the ladder of success. In the Old and Middle Kingdoms, only **noblemen** could hold high office.

Thutmose III is shown smiting Egypt's enemies.

The Egyptian Empire Expands

The term historians use to describe this period of warlike **expansion** is the New Kingdom (1558–1085 B.C.). Under Thutmose III, the Egyptian Empire spread into Syria and Palestine, where Egyptian armies clashed with rival empires for control of the Middle East. Thutmose III fought 17 military **campaigns** during his reign. To administer his empire, he brought nobles from the conquered territories to Egypt, where he educated and trained them. Then they returned to their homelands and governed as loyal servants of the pharaoh.

The chief **rivals** of the Egyptians were the Hittites. The two empires faced off in the **epic** battle of Kadesh. The 2,500 Hittite chariots of King Muwatalli clashed with a smaller number of Egyptian chariots, led by Ramses II. The large three-man chariots of the Hittites easily drove the light two-man Egyptian chariots before them. For a time, it seemed that the Egyptian army would be routed and all would be lost. The Hittites eventually broke off the battle to raid the Egyptian camp. When they did, the Egyptians counter-attacked and scattered the Hittite army. Many more years of warfare followed before the two sides finally decided upon peace. To finalize the agreement, Ramses even married a Hittite princess.

Ramses II at the Battle of Kadesh

Temple Building

The New Kingdom pharaohs were also great builders. Ramses II, the greatest of the builders, ordered the huge temple of **Abu Simbel** to be cut from the rock of a cliff overlooking the Nile. The Egyptians removed an estimated 365,000 tons of rock to create the structure. It was designed in such a way that on two mornings each year, 30 days before the spring **equinox** and 30 days after the autumnal equinox, the sun's rays could penetrate the 200 feet of darkness to light up the statues deep in the temple's interior. On either side of the doorway, four 67-foot statues of a seated Ramses were to guard the entrance.

Ramses II also made Thebes into an impressive capital city. He expanded the already huge temple to Amon-Re at Karnak to an area that covers over 200 acres. It was probably the largest religious structure ever built.

The huge statues at Abu Simbel represent Ramses II.

Egypt and the Middle East
The New Kingdom

Name: _____ Date: _____

Knowledge Check

Matching

____ 1. epic
____ 2. equinox
____ 3. noblemen
____ 4. expansion
____ 5. expel
____ 6. campaigns
____ 7. rival

a. the men distinguished by high birth or rank
b. the action of becoming larger
c. a competitor
d. one of the two times each year when there is an equal amount of daylight and darkness
e. a series of military operations
f. to extend beyond the usual or ordinary, especially in size or scope
g. to force someone out of a place or country

Multiple Choice

8. Which group of people did the New Kingdom drive from Egypt?
   a. Hittites
   b. Hyksos
   c. Syrians
   d. nobles

9. Which group of people were the Egyptians' main rivals for power in the Middle East?
   a. Hittites
   b. Hyksos
   c. Syrians
   d. nobles

10. In addition to war, for what were the New Kingdom pharaohs known?
    a. sailing
    b. running
    c. building
    d. writing

Constructed Response

11. Explain how the temple of Abu Simbel was built. Use at least two details form the selection to support your answer.

_____
_____
_____
_____
_____
_____
_____

Queen Hatshepsut

Divine Rulers

Because Egyptian pharaohs were considered **divine**, it was important for them to find divine wives. Since the only other divine beings in Egypt were in the royal family, pharaohs often married their sisters. One such sister and wife of a pharaoh was **Hatshepsut**. She, however, broke with tradition when her husband died and ruled as pharaoh in the place of her stepson, Thutmose III. She took on the official title "she who embraces Amun, the foremost of women."

This statue of Hatshepsut at her mortuary temple shows her wearing a ceremonial false beard.

The Pharaoh Queen

Throughout Egyptian history, many of the pharaohs' queens **wielded** equal power with their husbands, but none had been able to **seize** the throne and become pharaoh themselves. Not only was Hatshepsut the first woman to become pharaoh, but she was also the most successful until Cleopatra 1,400 years later.

Hatshepsut is known for her building program that included a huge and beautiful terraced **mortuary temple** at Deir-el-Bahri. Unlike most temples, it is open to the sun so that a visitor can study the 190 statues and carvings in the full light of day.

Hatshepsut is also famous for restoring Egypt to its former wealth by renewing foreign **commerce**. For example, in the ninth year of her reign, she sent five large cargo ships on a trading expedition to the land of Punt.

Hatshepsut proved to be an able ruler for about 20 years. By avoiding war where she could, she gave Egypt a breathing space in which it could recover its strength. Yet her position on the throne was not secure. As a woman, Egyptian law said that she technically could not rule as pharaoh. She tried to encourage her people to believe that she was a legitimate pharaoh by disguising her gender. She adopted the **ceremonial** false beard and masculine dress of male pharaohs. In some of her **inscriptions** she even calls herself "His Majesty."

Thutmose III

Her stepson, Thutmose III, had been declared pharaoh before Hatshepsut seized the throne. As he grew into manhood, his impatience and resentment toward the strong-willed woman increased. Finally, he gathered the supporters that he needed and overthrew the queen. We do not know the details of this event, but it is likely that Hatshepsut was killed as a result.

Thutmose III tried to undo all that his stepmother had accomplished. He abandoned peaceful relations with neighboring countries and launched attacks into Nubia and Palestine. He also destroyed Hatshepsut's statues and erased her name from all the temples and monuments that she had constructed during her reign.

Thutmose III

Egypt and the Middle East

Queen Hatshepsut

Name: _____ Date: _____

Knowledge Check

Matching

_____ 1. seize
_____ 2. mortuary temple
_____ 3. divine
_____ 4. commerce
_____ 5. wield
_____ 6. inscription
_____ 7. ceremonial

a. the exchange or buying and selling of items on a large scale
b. to capture by using force
c. to use power or influence
d. the wording on a monument or in a book
e. to be like a god
f. the system of rules to be observed at a formal or religious occasion
g. a place set aside for the worship of a deceased pharaoh

Multiple Choice

8. How long did Hatshepsut rule?
   a. about 20 years
   b. about 25 years
   c. about 30 years
   d. about 35 years

9. Who was the stepson of Hatshepsut?
   a. Deir-el-Bahri
   b. Thutmose V
   c. Amun
   d. Thutmose III

10. What is remarkable about Deir-el-Bahri?
    a. It is open to the sun.
    b. It was open all night.
    c. It is closed to the sun.
    d. It was very small.

Critical Thinking

11. What conclusions can you draw about Hatshepsut's personality? Support your answer with examples or details from the reading selection.

_____
_____
_____
_____
_____
_____

Akhenaton the Bizarre

Amenhotep IV or Akhenaton

One of the most extraordinary and mysterious pharaohs in Egyptian history is Amenhotep IV. His statues show a **grotesque** figure. Archaeologists have come up with many possible explanations for Amenhotep's remarkable physical characteristics. Some say that he suffered from a glandular disorder that deformed his body. Others say that he wanted to emphasize his closeness with a creator god.

Early in his reign, he clashed with the powerful **priests** of the god **Amon-Re**, known as the king of the gods. Amenhotep IV replaced the god Amon-Re with a new god called **Aton**, the solar disc. The pharaoh even changed his own name from Amenhotep, which honored Amon-Re, to **Akhenaton**, which meant "pleasant to Aton."

The Amarna Period

Historians refer to Akhenaton's reign as the **Amarna period**. It gets its name from Amarna, the modern name for the location of the pharaoh's new city on the edge of the desert. The ancient Egyptians called it **Akhetaton**. The new city saw fascinating times. By piecing together surviving fragments of literature and sculpture from the period, archaeologists have come to believe that Akhenaton was motivated by more than just jealousy of the priests of Amon-Re. The fragments show an intense devotion to Aton as a **benevolent** god of all nations, not just Egypt. Worship of all other gods was discouraged. Because of this, Akhenaton is often called the first **monotheist** in history. A monotheist is someone who worships only one god. In fact, it was more complicated than that. Akhenaton himself was worshipped as a god, and the Egyptian people could only worship Aton through the pharaoh.

Akhenaton and His Wife Nefertiti

The Amarna period is also known for more **realistic** art forms than before. Egyptian artists for the first time tried to create more natural and life-like images. Artists painted ordinary scenes of plants and animals seen along the Nile. Akhenaton ordered the court sculptors to break with tradition of portraying the pharaoh as expressionless and remote or god-like.

Realistic Art From a Wall at Amarna

The writings of the time also show a new creativity. Akhenaton introduced everyday language and **idiomatic** expressions into literature. Egyptian poets experimented with new expressions and ideas.

Despite Akhenaton's efforts, he ultimately failed. His **veneration** of Aton did not survive him. When he died, the priests of Amon-Re quickly re-established control. The name of Akhenaton and his god Aton were hammered out. His city was abandoned to the desert. To the next pharaoh, Akhenaton left a very weakened and confused Egypt.

Egypt and the Middle East | Akhenaton the Bizarre

Name: _____ Date: _____

Knowledge Check

Matching

_____ 1. priests   a. to regard with respect
_____ 2. grotesque   b. sayings peculiar to or characteristic of a given language
_____ 3. monotheist   c. members of the clergy; those who lead others in worship
_____ 4. realistic   d. a person who worships only one god
_____ 5. veneration   e. the representation of things as they really are
_____ 6. idiomatic   f. to organize for the purpose of doing good
_____ 7. benevolent   g. a very ugly or distorted figure, creature, or image

Multiple Choice

8. What was the name of Amenhotep IV's new god?
   a. Amon-Re   b. Akhenaton
   c. Amarna   d. Aton

9. What was Amenhotep IV's new name?
   a. Amarna   b. Akhenaton
   c. Amon-Re   d. Aton

10. What do historians call the reign of Amenhotep?
    a. the Amarna period   b. the Akhenaton period
    c. the Aton period   d. the Amon-Re period

Constructed Response

11. Archaeologists have come up with many possible explanations for Amenhotep's odd physical characteristics. List two, using details from the selection to support your answer.

_____
_____
_____
_____
_____
_____
_____

The Tomb of Tutankhamen

This small coffin held Tutankhamen's mummified liver.

Unlike the rest of the New Kingdom pharaohs, Tutankhamen's tomb eluded **grave robbers**, leaving it almost intact to be discovered by Howard Carter in 1922. It remains as probably the world's most exciting archaeological discovery.

The Reign of Tutankhamen

Upon Akhenaton's death, Egypt was thrown into **turmoil** for a few years. Finally, order was partially restored when Akhenaton's ten-year-old son-in-law was crowned pharaoh. He took the name **Tutankhamen**. Under the new king, the priests of Amon-Re re-established their authority. The worship of Aton was **abolished**, and Akhenaton's city was abandoned. The temples to Aton were **dismantled** and the materials shipped across the river to build new temples to Amon-Re. The power of the Amon-Re **priesthood** was never again challenged.

Tutankhamen was known as the boy king.

Tutankhamen's reign lasted only nine years, and he was buried, like the rest of the New Kingdom pharaohs, in the Valley of the Kings. The **mummy** of Tutankhamen reveals that he probably died from a genetic bone disease and malaria. He probably had weak, brittle bones. At the same time that he was battling malaria, he fell and broke his leg. The illness and injury combined to kill him. In any case, his death was **premature** because he left no heirs. His widow, Ankhesenamun, desperately tried to maintain order by finding another husband. She appealed to the Hittite king Suppiluliumas to send one of his sons to marry her and become pharaoh. The Hittite prince made it only as far as the Egyptian border where he was mysteriously murdered. Ankhesenamun apparently lost control and a period of instability followed.

Ramses II

Eventually, a new **dynasty** was established when a military commander named Ramses II seized the throne. The next pharaoh, Ramses III, successfully fought off a dangerous invasion of the so-called Sea Peoples, whom historians believe were probably early Greeks.

By the end of Ramses III's reign, however, Egypt was in decline. The costs of maintaining a huge army, building **monumental** temples, and keeping the priests of Amon-Re content were draining the pharaoh's treasury. Grave robbing had become so bad that a number of mummies from the Valley of the Kings had been removed and placed in a common tomb where they could be better guarded. After the death of Ramses III, eight more pharaohs ruled with the name Ramses as Egypt slid into chaos. Finally, a **succession** of foreign invaders swept into Egypt and battled amongst themselves for control. The Libyans were first, but they were overthrown by the Nubians, who were overthrown by the Assyrians. Egypt, the home of an ancient and magnificent civilization, by the eighth century B.C., was merely a **province** of somebody else's empire.

Egypt and the Middle East

The Tomb of Tutankhamen

Name: _____ Date: _____

Knowledge Check

Matching

_____ 1. turmoil
_____ 2. dynasty
_____ 3. abolished
_____ 4. priesthood
_____ 5. mummy
_____ 6. premature
_____ 7. dismantled
_____ 8. monumental

a. before the proper or usual time
b. a line of rulers from one family
c. to put an end to
d. a state of great disturbance, confusion, or uncertainty
e. the office or position of a priest
f. to take apart or tear down
g. to be great in importance, extent, or size
h. a dead body that has been prepared for burial in the manner of the ancient Egyptians

Multiple Choice

9. Where was Tutankhamen's tomb located?
   a. The Valley of the Queens
   b. Libya
   c. The Valley of the Kings
   d. Amon-Re's temple

10. How long was Tutankhamen pharaoh?
    a. nine years
    b. nineteen years
    c. twelve years
    d. three years

11. When was the tomb of Tutankhamen discovered?
    a. 1923   b. 1912   c. 1902   d. 1922

Constructed Response

12. Explain what happened during Tutankhamen's reign. Use two details from the selection to support your answer.

_____
_____
_____
_____
_____
_____
_____

The Rise and Fall of Empires in the Middle East

The Hittites

With their mighty chariots, the Hittites conquered most of the **Middle East**, except for Egypt. The Hittites were more than just horsemen and conquerors, however. They borrowed **cuneiform** writing from the Babylonians to keep detailed records and preserve hymns and myths. They also built a beautiful capital city at Hattusa in **Anatolia**, which is part of modern-day Turkey.

Relief Showing 12 Hittite Gods of the Underworld at Hattusa

From Hattusa, the Hittite kings administered their empire through a surprisingly **humane law code**. Instead of following the old Babylonian law codes that required an eye for an eye, the Hittite laws were based on **restitution**. Arsonists were required to replace property that they set afire. Murderers could go free after they paid the family of the victim a large amount of silver, slaves, or land. Hittite society was **feudal**. Nobles held land from the king in return for promises of troops and chariots in time of war. Yet, after only 500 years, Hattusa was attacked by the mysterious Sea Peoples and destroyed, along with most of its population.

The Assyrian Empire

The Middle East wasn't to be without an **empire** for long. The Assyrian Empire stepped into the space once filled by the Hittites. They came from the northern part of Mesopotamia. Their empire, however, was far different. Their chief **deity** was Ashur, the god of war. As a result, they were interested only in preserving tradition and the arts and sciences of armed conflict. Instead of law codes, the Assyrians relied on terror and intimidation to control the Middle East. Many of those who had suffered under Assyrian control rose up and destroyed the empire.

The Persian Empire

The last and greatest Middle Eastern empire of the ancient world was that of the Persians. Their home was in modern-day Iran, but their empire stretched from the Indus Valley across the Middle East to include Egypt and the Ionian coast. The Persian kings, beginning with their founder Cyrus, ruled with wisdom and toleration. The Persians respected local traditions and honored the local gods. They tried to interfere as little as possible with the affairs of the people within their empire.

A descendant of Cyrus, Darius, constructed a great capital at Persepolis. The Persian builders

Drawing of the Palace of Darius I of Persia at Persepolis

borrowed architectural styles from all over the Middle East. The city was built on **terraces** like Babylon. Its walls were decorated with **reliefs** of Assyrian human-headed bulls. The doorways looked like those found in Egyptian temples. Finally, columns from far-off Greece held up the roof of the audience hall. At the time, Darius would never have dreamt that the Greeks would someday come to dominate the **political** and **cultural** life of Persia.

Egypt and the Middle East

The Rise and Fall of Empires in the Middle East

Name: _____ Date: _____

Knowledge Check

Matching

_____ 1. humane law code
_____ 2. feudal
_____ 3. cuneiform
_____ 4. terraces
_____ 5. empire
_____ 6. deity
_____ 7. cultural

a. the ideas, customs, and social behavior of a society
b. leveled platforms of earth built into a hillside
c. the territory under the authority of a single ruler
d. system where nobles held land from the king in return for promises of troops and chariots in time of war
e. a god or goddess
f. a set of laws based on restitution
g. a system of writing used by the Babylonians

Multiple Choice

8. Where was the location of the Hittite capital Hattusa?
   a. Greece
   b. Anatolia
   c. Italy
   d. Persia

9. How did the Assyrians maintain control of their empire?
   a. by humane law code
   b. by terror
   c. by slavery
   d. by law of the land

10. Which was the last and greatest of the Middle Eastern empires?
    a. Greece
    b. Persia
    c. Hattusa
    d. Turkey

Constructed Response

11. Explain how the Hittite law code differed from the Babylonian. Use details from the selection to support your answer.

_____

_____

_____

_____

_____

_____

_____

The Creative Nations of Phoenicia and Israel

The Phoenicians

The **Phoenicians** were the first great **navigators** of the Middle East. They developed solid ocean-going vessels that could ride the Mediterranean Sea when it turned stormy. These ships could carry in their holds cargo to be traded throughout the Middle East, North Africa, and the coasts of Europe. They learned to navigate these ships by the stars.

The Phoenicians left other **legacies**. In order to make trade easier, they came up with a simple **alphabet** of 22 symbols. In modified form, this later became the alphabet that you're reading right now. The Phoenicians also left colonies all over the Mediterranean that later turned into important cities like Palermo, Cadiz, and Carthage. Finally, they took the knowledge of weaving, glassmaking, and **metallurgy** developed by their neighbors in the Middle East and spread it throughout the ancient world.

Example of Phoenician Writing

The Hebrews

Another small nation that had a large impact was that of the **Hebrews**. We know a great deal about the history of the Hebrews because it makes up much of the first half of the **Bible**, known to Christians as the Old Testament. The Hebrews developed a monotheistic religion. **Monotheism** is a belief in one god. Central to their religion was the belief that they had a **covenant** with God, whom they called **Yahweh** or Jehovah. They believed that they were to worship and be obedient to him alone, and that in return he would bring blessings to them.

At first, the Hebrews were wandering **nomads**, but eventually they were enslaved in Egypt. Under the guidance of Moses, they fled into Sinai. After many years they at last entered the promised land of Canaan. There they defeated the local population, called the Canaanites. For two centuries their kingdom thrived. Under King Solomon, they enjoyed a golden age. Solomon acquired cedar logs from the Phoenicians and built a huge temple for Yahweh at Jerusalem.

When Solomon died, however, the Hebrews split into separate kingdoms, called Israel and Judah. In 722 B.C., the Assyrians captured much of Israel, and a century and a half later, Jerusalem (the capital of Judah) was destroyed by the Chaldeans. Many Hebrews were marched off to Babylonia. From this point on, the Hebrews were known as **Jews**.

When they were, at last, allowed to return to their homeland and rebuild the temple at Jerusalem, they had become a tight-knit community that stressed law, ritual, and tradition. They preserved their traditions in two important collections of books. These are called the *Talmud*, or instructions, and the *Torah*, which recorded the early history and laws of the Jewish people.

King Solomon Dedicating the Temple at Jerusalem

Egypt and the Middle East · The Creative Nations of Phoenicia and Israel

Name: _____ Date: _____

Knowledge Check

Matching

_____ 1. *Torah*
_____ 2. legacy
_____ 3. nomads
_____ 4. Jews
_____ 5. navigators
_____ 6. metallurgy
_____ 7. monotheism

a. the people who plot a route for water travel
b. the first five books of the Hebrew scriptures
c. a thing handed down by an ancestor or predecessor
d. a people who have no permanent home and wander from place to place to find fresh pasture for their livestock
e. the branch of science that deals with the properties of metals
f. a group of people whose religion is Judaism
g. a belief in one god

Phoenician Statue Made of Bronze and Covered With Gold

Multiple Choice

8. What did the Phoenicians invent to make trade easier?
   a. metallurgy
   b. glassmaking
   c. a number system
   d. an alphabet

9. What were the names of the two Hebrew kingdoms?
   a. Israel and Judah
   b. Palermo and Cadiz
   c. Israel and Carthage
   d. Jerusalem and Sinai

10. When did the Hebrews become known as Jews?
    a. before Solomon died
    b. when they were marched off to Babylon
    c. when the king decreed it
    d. when they voted on it

Constructed Response

11. Explain how the Phoenicians helped spread Middle Eastern civilization. Use at least two details from the selection to support your answer.

_____
_____
_____
_____
_____
_____
_____

Alexander the Great Conquers His World

Alexander had **inherited** the powerful kingdom of Macedonia from his father, Philip II. Under Philip's leadership, Macedonia began to absorb much of the advanced Greek civilization. Greece, however, was not a single state but many warring **city-states**. Philip took advantage of these divisions to bring most of Greece under his control. Having achieved this, he decided to attack Persia. Before he could launch his attack, he was **assassinated**.

Alexander at the Battle of Gaugamela Where He Defeated Darius III

Alexander Marches East

Alexander was no ordinary 20-year-old when he inherited the throne of Macedonia. He was not only determined to carry on what his father had begun, but he also wanted to unite the known world under his power. First, he **conquered** Egypt and founded a new city called Alexandria. This became the most important city in Alexander's empire. Next, he defeated the Persian emperor, Darius III. Alexander was declared to be the new Persian emperor. Even with the whole Middle East at his feet, Alexander was not yet satisfied. He marched his army east to the **sacred** river of India, the Indus. Here, he met and defeated the war elephants of Porus, the king of the Punjab.

By this time, however, Alexander's men were weary of their **conquests** and were homesick. Alexander at last began the long journey back. The trip was incredibly difficult, and three-quarters of his men perished along the way because of exhaustion and lack of water.

At last he arrived in Susa. Here, to symbolize the union of the Greek and Middle Eastern parts of his empire, he presided over a mass wedding. Eighty of his officers married eighty Persian women. Alexander himself married Stateira, the daughter of Darius. He later traveled to Babylonia to supervise the building of a new temple and make plans to explore the Caspian Sea. While there, he fell ill with fever and died. He was 33 years old.

The Hellenistic Era

Alexander's empire did not last long. Soon his generals were fighting among themselves for control. Nevertheless, he had a profound influence on the Middle East. He left an exciting new civilization that mixed ideas from Greece with the dramatically different approaches to life that he found from Egypt to India. This civilization is called **Hellenistic**. The 300 years after the death of Alexander when the new civilization flourished is called the Hellenistic era. It was a time of great toleration and open-mindedness when different cultures could freely mix. There were many great achievements in art, philosophy, and science. The cultural environment also opened up opportunities for new trade between lands very far and different from each other.

This piece of jewelry shows a Hellenistic king as Ares the Greek god of war.

Egypt and the Middle East Alexander the Great Conquers His World

Name: _____ Date: _____

Knowledge Check

Matching

_____ 1. inherit
_____ 2. Hellenistic
_____ 3. conquests
_____ 4. sacred
_____ 5. conquered
_____ 6. assassinated
_____ 7. city-state

a. to be murdered for political reasons
b. connected or associated with God
c. to be defeated by force
d. to come into possession of money, property, or a title as an heir at the death of the previous holder
e. mixture of ideas from Greece with those in the Middle East
f. acts of conquering
g. unit of government based around a city

Multiple Choice

8. How old was Alexander when he set out to conquer the world?
   a. 30   b. 19   c. 20   d. 21

9. How old was Alexander when he died?
   a. 33   b. 43   c. 53   d. 64

10. What was the most important city in Alexander's empire?
    a. Athens   b. Susa
    c. Babylonia   d. Alexandria

11. Who was the Persian emperor defeated by Alexander?
    a. Philip II   b. Darius III
    c. Stateira   d. Porus

Constructed Response

12. Explain why the Hellenistic era was a time of toleration and open-mindedness. Use details from the selection to support your answer.

_____
_____
_____
_____
_____
_____

The Middle East and the Roman Empire

The Roman Empire

As the Roman fleet attacked the Egyptian warships, Queen Cleopatra's ship fled, leaving Antony behind. Within a year, the Roman forces occupied Egypt. To avoid capture, Queen Cleopatra and Antony committed suicide. Egypt became just another province of the Roman Empire.

Like Egypt, the other warring kingdoms in the Middle East that succeeded the empire of Alexander the Great were easy prey for the new empire of the Romans. Rome started out as a small village dominated by neighboring powers. In time, the Romans dominated Italy and then the whole Mediterranean.

From 29 B.C. to A.D. 14, most of the Middle East except for Persia and part of Mesopotamia

The Roman General Antony Joins Egyptian Queen Cleopatra on Her Barge

also came under Roman control. The Roman emperors allowed cooperative local kings to keep their thrones. The new empire offered security from attack under Rome's unbeatable armed forces, as well as efficient government and stability. For several centuries the Middle East settled down to enjoy the **Pax Romana**, or the Roman Peace. The rich Hellenistic culture left behind by Alexander the Great also made it easy for the Middle East to accept Roman domination. The Romans themselves had borrowed much of their culture from Hellenistic Greece. Most Roman art, philosophy, and architecture had their origins in Greek styles and ideas.

Roman General Titus

Jews Revolt

Not all people of the Middle East were happy with Roman rule. After Caligula decided to make himself a god, everyone accepted it except the **Jews**. The Jews revolted and refused to bow to Caligula's statues at Alexandria. This led to an attack on Jews. The Roman general Titus attacked Jerusalem in A.D. 70, killing thousands. Their temple was destroyed with only the west wall (known as the **Wailing Wall** today) remaining.

In 132, another revolt broke out that lasted over three years. Many of the Jews were killed, sold into slavery, or forced to leave Jerusalem. Many went to Galilee. Eventually, a Jewish ruler called the **ethnarch** was appointed. That seemed to solve the problem, and for 200 years there were no revolts.

The long period of exile from their homeland and **persecution** is known in Jewish history as the **Diaspora**. The Jews who fled Jerusalem went in many directions: to Europe, North Africa, and the Middle East. A major center for Jews was Baghdad. There, Jewish scholars were trained in academies, and study of the *Talmud* (Jewish law) continued. A thriving community remained until the **Muslims** swept into the region in the seventh century. Others moved to Europe where some Jews had already located. After the breakup of the Roman Empire, they came under **Christian** rule. Some converted to Christianity, but others kept their faith. The most influential Jewish community in Europe was in Spain.

Egypt and the Middle East   The Middle East and the Roman Empire

Name: _____ Date: _____

Knowledge Check

Matching

_____ 1. exile
_____ 2. ethnarch
_____ 3. Wailing Wall
_____ 4. Diaspora
_____ 5. Muslims
_____ 6. persecution
_____ 7. Pax Romana

a. a Jewish ruler appointed by the Romans
b. the scattering of Jews to many parts of the world
c. a period of peace for the Roman Empire that lasted around 200 years
d. a policy of arresting, injuring, or killing members of a religious or ethnic group
e. the followers of the religion of Islam
f. an enforced removal from one's native country
g. a remnant of the western retaining wall of the second Temple in Jerusalem

Multiple Choice

8. How did Cleopatra avoid capture?
   a. She fled to Spain.
   b. She committed suicide.
   c. She disguised herself.
   d. She hid in a secret bunker.

9. Where did the Romans get many of their ideas in art, philosophy, and architecture?
   a. the English
   b. the Spaniards
   c. the Egyptians
   d. the Greeks

10. What do we call the west wall today?
    a. the Wailing Wall
    b. the Wishing Wall
    c. the Wall of Prayer
    d. the Prayer Wall

Constructed Response

11. Explain what happened to the Jews during the Diaspora. Use at least two details from the selection to support your answer.

_____
_____
_____
_____
_____
_____
_____

Christianity Conquers Rome

A New Religion

Christianity is a religion founded in Judea about 2,000 years ago. It grew out of the teachings of **Jesus** of Nazareth. Historians and religious scholars rely on the first four books of the **New Testament**, which are called the **Gospels**, for information about his life. From these we learn that Jesus was born to a Jewish family. At about age 30, he began to preach a message of love and forgiveness that minimized the old rituals and laws of the Jews. While some accepted his message, most did not because it differed from conventional Jewish wisdom and practice. Eventually, the Jewish authorities in Palestine saw him as a threat to the peace because crowds began to proclaim him as king, or **Messiah**. They feared that the Romans would interpret this as a sign of revolt. Jesus was arrested and turned over to the Roman governor, Pontius Pilate. He somewhat reluctantly ordered Jesus' death by **crucifixion**.

During the days and weeks after his death, Jesus's followers reported seeing and talking to him. They proclaimed him the Messiah and announced that he would soon return to establish the kingdom of Heaven on Earth. They fanned out and told others about him. Christianity spread throughout the eastern Mediterranean and all the way to Rome.

This shows Roman governor Pontius Pilate washing his hands to signify he was not responsible for the death of Jesus.

Christianity Spreads

At first, the Christians suffered persecution at the hands of Roman officials. Nevertheless, the religion continued to thrive and many people were converted throughout the Middle East and North Africa. Eventually, the Roman emperors themselves converted to Christianity

During this time, the Roman Empire was in decline. Uncivilized tribes from the north called **barbarians** began to threaten the borders. Meanwhile, high taxes, plagues, and civil wars disrupted life within the empire. As a result, Emperor Diocletian decided that the empire was too big for one man to rule. He divided it into two parts, an Eastern and a Western Roman Empire. The **Eastern Empire** included most of the Middle East and North Africa.

When Constantine became emperor, he founded a new capital for the Eastern Empire at Byzantium in present-day Turkey. He named his new capital Constantinople. Here the traditions and authority of the Roman Empire were preserved for a thousand years. Byzantium also became heir to Hellenistic and Middle Eastern culture. Therefore, **Byzantine civilization** is different from Roman. Long after Rome fell in the West, the Middle East continued to enjoy the benefits of a rich and creative Christian civilization that combined the best of East and West.

Emperor Constantine is shown with a model of the city of Constantinople in this mosaic from the Hagia Sophia in what is now Istanbul.

Egypt and the Middle East

Christianity Conquers Rome

Name: _____ Date: _____

Knowledge Check

Matching

____ 1. Jesus
____ 2. Messiah
____ 3. Byzantine civilization
____ 4. New Testament
____ 5. barbarians
____ 6. Christianity
____ 7. crucifixion

a. culture that developed in the Eastern Roman Empire, centered around Constantinople, with elements of Roman, Hellenistic, and Middle Eastern culture
b. a religion founded in Judea about 2,000 years ago
c. an execution on a cross
d. the second part of the Bible containing the Gospels, which tell about the life of Jesus
e. uncivilized tribes from north of the Roman Empire
f. a teacher and prophet; his life and sermons formed the basis for Christianity
g. a special leader the Jewish people believe will be sent by God to guide them and set up God's rule on Earth

Multiple Choice

8. Who divided the Roman Empire in half?
   a. Constantine
   b. Pontius Pilate
   c. Diocletian
   d. Jesus

9. What was the name of the new capital of the Eastern Roman Empire?
   a. Palestine
   b. Judea
   c. Rome
   d. Constantinople

10. Which Roman governor ordered the death of Jesus by crucifixion?
    a. Pontius Pilate
    b. Diocletian
    c. Constantine
    d. Byzantine

Constructed Response

11. Explain why the Roman Empire was divided into two parts. Use details from the selection to support your answer.

_____
_____
_____
_____
_____
_____

From the Sands of Arabia Comes Islam

A New Religion Comes From Mecca

Around A.D. 610, **Muhammad** founded the religion of **Islam**. Muhammad was born in the Arabian town of Mecca. His teachings were written in the **Koran** (*Qur'an*). He taught there was a special place in heaven for those who died for their faith. When the leader or **caliph** called for a Holy War called a **jihad**, the loyal follower's duty was to respond.

Islam shares many of the beliefs of Judaism and Christianity. In fact, many of the early leaders and prophets like Abraham and Moses are also held in high esteem by Muslims and are found in the *Koran*. The Muslims also believe in only one God, whom they call Allah. The *Koran* also mentions Jesus but sees him as a **prophet**, like Muhammad.

The Five Pillars of Islam

The *Koran* requires Muslims to follow the five pillars of Islam. The first pillar is the **Shahadah**. Muslims must say and believe that there is no God but Allah and Muhammad is his messenger. The second pillar is **Salat**. Five times a day, a good Muslim should face Mecca, bathe his face, arms, feet, and hands, and recite prayers. On Friday at noon, all Muslims should gather at the **mosque** and pray together. The third pillar is **Sawm**. Each year during the month of **Ramadan**, Muslims must neither eat nor drink from sunrise to sunset. When the sun sets, Muslim families gather to celebrate Ramadan with feasts of specially prepared and delicious food. The fourth pillar of Islam is **Zakat**. All Muslims must pay part of their income to help provide for the poor. The fifth pillar of Islam is **Hajj**. At least once in a Muslim's life, he or she should make the journey to Mecca. Here he or she performs certain rituals established by Muhammad. These include circling the **Ka'ba**, an ancient stone enclosure, which the Muslims believe was rebuilt by Abraham; stoning a pillar that represents the Devil; and gathering on the plains of Arafat where Muhammad gave his last sermon. Today, millions of Muslims from all over the world come to Mecca on Hajj.

Visiting the sacred stone in Mecca called the Ka'ba is part of the Hajj, the fifth pillar of Islam.

Islam Spreads Throughout the Middle East

At first, most of the people of Mecca laughed at Muhammad and believed he was insane. Nevertheless, in time he gathered about him a group of followers who believed him to be the messenger of God. As the number of Muhammad's followers increased, he became a threat to the rulers of Mecca. His enemies even attempted to assassinate him. He was forced to seek shelter in the nearby city of Medina. Here, he won over the inhabitants by settling a dangerous dispute that divided the city. The Meccans sent armies to defeat Muhammad's followers, but they were defeated in battle after battle. Eventually, Muhammad was able to return to Mecca in triumph. While still alive, Muhammad's message spread all over Arabia. Upon his death in 632, the new religion was carried throughout the Middle East.

Egypt and the Middle East
From the Sands of Arabia Comes Islam

Name: _____ Date: _____

Knowledge Check

Matching

_____ 1. mosque
_____ 2. prophet
_____ 3. caliph
_____ 4. Ka'ba
_____ 5. Muhammad
_____ 6. *Koran*
_____ 7. Ramadan

a. a Muslim leader who had both political and religious authority
b. the founder of Islam
c. the sacred text of Islam
d. a Muslim place of worship
e. a sacred Muslim shrine in Mecca
f. a person regarded as an inspired teacher of the will of God
g. the holy month when Muslims observe strict fasting from sunrise to sunset

Multiple Choice

8. What is the name of the first pillar of Islam?
   a. Shahadah
   b. Salat
   c. Sawm
   d. Hajj

9. What is the name of the fifth pillar of Islam?
   a. Hajj
   b. Zakat
   c. Salat
   d. Shahadah

10. What is the name of the third pillar of Islam?
    a. Sawm
    b. Hajj
    c. Zakat
    d. Salat

Constructed Response

11. Which Islamic beliefs are shared with Judaism and Christianity? Explain your answer using details from the selection.

_____
_____
_____
_____
_____
_____

The Islamic Golden Age

Islam Spreads

Upon the death of Muhammad, **Islam** spread throughout the Middle East at great speed. Within 200 years after the prophet's death, an Islamic empire spread from Iran in the east to Spain in the west. For a time, all of this was united under the control of the caliph in Baghdad. **Caliph** means successor to Muhammad, and it was under these men that the new religion spread.

The Persian scientist al-Razi was a physician.

Islam expanded quickly for many reasons. First, the Arabs were great warriors and were led by brilliant generals like Khalid ibn-al-Walid. They believed they were fighting a **jihad**, or holy war. Secondly, many people in the Middle East were weary of Byzantine control. The Byzantine Empire imposed heavy taxes and was intolerant of the many splinter groups that had grown up within Christianity. The Orthodox Byzantine emperors called these groups **heresies** and tried to crush them by force. Finally, the Byzantine Empire was exhausted by warfare against the other great power of the Middle East, Persia. As a result, all of Persia and all of the Byzantine Empire except Turkey quickly fell to the caliph's warriors.

The Golden Age of Islam

After the Islamic conquest, the Middle East enjoyed a new golden age under Islam. All trade routes between Europe, Asia, and Africa passed through the Middle East. Muslim cities like Baghdad, Cairo, and Basra became thriving trade centers. In particular, the wealth and magnificence of Baghdad became legendary. Also, non-Arabic peoples like the Persians and Egyptians were gradually merged into the empire.

From the eighth to the 12th centuries, the Muslim world was a place of scholarship, scientific learning, and artistic creativity. Scholars translated and studied Greek and Persian books on philosophy, astronomy, chemistry, physics, geography, and medicine. Al-Razi, a Persian scientist, was the first physician to use plaster casts to set bones. He also accurately described the symptoms of diseases like smallpox and measles. Muslim scholar al-Idrisi revolutionized geography by creating maps representing the spherical shape of the earth.

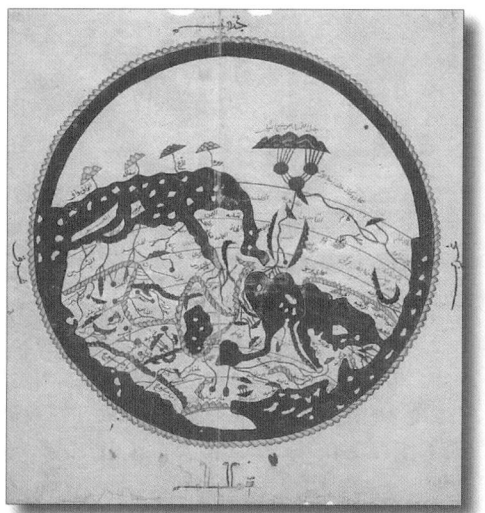

Al-Idrisi's World Map With South at the Top of the Map

Islamic art and architecture included objects of breathtaking beauty. As in the sciences, the Muslims borrowed from Byzantium, Persia, and even China. Yet, they went beyond these influences to **synthesize** and develop their own styles. Islam forbade pictures or statues of natural objects like animals and people. To compensate, Muslim artists created exquisite **geometric** designs to decorate their mosques. They also took the art of beautiful handwriting, called **calligraphy**, and developed it into graceful and elegant decoration.

Egypt and the Middle East — The Islamic Golden Age

Name: _____ Date: _____

Knowledge Check

Matching

_____ 1. Islam
_____ 2. calligraphy
_____ 3. heresies
_____ 4. synthesize
_____ 5. jihad
_____ 6. geometric
_____ 7. caliph

a. a holy war undertaken as a sacred duty by Muslims
b. using figures from geometry such as lines, circles, and shapes
c. a Muslim leader who had both political and religious authority
d. the religion of Muslims based on the teachings of the prophet Muhammad
e. to create or develop
f. the Arabic handwriting designed in an artistic style
g. Christian groups who had opinions not accepted by the Roman Catholic Church

Multiple Choice

8. Who was the Persian physician who used plaster casts to set bones?
   a. Khalid ibn-al-Walid
   b. al-Idrisi
   c. al-Razi
   d. Suleiman

9. Who changed geography by creating maps showing the earth as a sphere?
   a. al-Razi
   b. Khalid ibn-al-Walid
   c. Suleiman
   d. al-Idrisi

10. The caliph was what to Muhammad?
    a. successor
    b. destroyer
    c. champion
    d. happiness

Constructed Response

11. Explain why Islam spread throughout the Middle East so quickly. Use details from the selection to support your answer.

_____
_____
_____
_____
_____
_____
_____

Crusaders Descend Upon the Middle East

Capturing the Holy City

The blistering heat of the summer sun made the armor of the **Crusaders** too hot to touch and miserable to wear. Yet, here they stood, outside Jerusalem, the **Holy City** itself. The Muslim defenders appeared to be weakening. The order was given again to advance. Down the dusty slopes of their **earthworks** the Crusaders pushed the **battering ram**. Others carried ladders to mount the walls. They were met by arrows and rocks from the defenders on the walls. This time, however, the gate gave way and the attackers, sensing victory, found new strength to push into the city itself. The long years of fighting, illness, and fatigue seemed to be coming to an end. To taste success at last after so much frustration put the Crusaders into a frenzy. The Crusaders celebrated the capture of the Holy City by massacring most of its inhabitants—Muslim, Christian, and Jew.

Crusaders Fighting in the Holy Land

The capture of Jerusalem, as described above, was only one episode in a series of European invasions of the Middle East that historians call the **Crusades**. For many centuries before the Crusades, the Christian Church in Europe had battled for survival against **pagans** and even Christian kings. By the 11th century, the church had emerged stronger than ever. At this point the Byzantine Emperor, Alexius Comnenus I, sent envoys to the pope in Rome requesting help. Byzantium was being threatened by a new and aggressive tribe from Central Asia called the **Seljuk Turks**. After converting to Islam, they conquered much of the Middle East and hoped to absorb the remnants of the Byzantine Empire. Alexius Comnenus I requested military support to help defend his **realm** and protect Christians who wanted to go on pilgrimage to Jerusalem and lands nearby where **Jesus** had lived. **Pilgrimage**, or visiting holy places, was an important feature of medieval Christianity.

The First Crusade

Pope Urban II called on all of Christian Europe to embark on a holy Crusade, or holy war, against the **infidels**, as the Christians called all Muslims. The support for the Crusade was tremendous. Soon, men from all over France, Italy, and Sicily were sewing crosses on their clothing and marching off to war. Historians estimate that in the first Crusade somewhere between 5,000 and 10,000 mounted **knights**, between 25,000 and 50,000 foot soldiers, and as many more wives, servants, families, and religious men set out for the Holy Land. Why did they go? There were many reasons. Many were filled with genuine religious zeal to recapture Jerusalem. Others, however, sought adventure and wealth. Many poor or landless knights hoped to make themselves lords or even princes.

The Crusaders encountered many unforeseen difficulties on their long journey to Palestine. Beginning in northern France, some marched overland through Germany, Hungary, and Bulgaria to Constantinople. One of the first groups, led by Peter the Hermit, was so badly organized that by the time they reached Bulgaria, they had to prey on fellow Christians for food. As a result, they were attacked and many were killed. When the remnants were **ferried** across the **Bosporus** by the Byzantine Emperor, they were easily massacred or captured and sold into slavery by the Turks. A second group made up of knights and soldiers led by Godfrey of Bouillon had more success. Because it was an organized army, it arrived in Byzantium intact and went on to attack Seljuk Turkish strongholds. Finally, after a long, bloody fight, Godfrey of Bouillon and his soldiers captured Jerusalem on July 5, 1099.

After accomplishing their objective, some Crusaders went home, but others stayed to establish **Crusader states** and live off their conquered wealth. Godfrey of Bouillon was named king of the Latin Kingdom of Jerusalem. Others became lords or **counts**. However, Christian control of Palestine was brief. Within fifty years, the Crusader states were fighting amongst themselves. After recovering from the shock of the first Crusade, Muslim warriors took advantage of these divisions to begin to win back lost territory. Finally, Saladin, one of the greatest and wisest of the Muslim princes, attacked and recaptured Jerusalem.

Godfrey of Bouillon

Results of the Crusades

Many more Crusades were called over the course of the next century but all failed to win more than token victories. In fact, they tended to weaken Christian control of Byzantium. The Fourth Crusade allowed itself to be distracted by the promise of Constantinople's wealth and captured the city from the Christian Byzantines in 1204. Although the Byzantines later regained control, the empire was permanently weakened and finally fell to the Turks in 1453.

The Crusades failed to **conquer** the Holy Land for Christian Europe, but they had far-reaching consequences. First, it exposed Europeans to the advances in philosophy, technology, medicine, and mathematics of the Muslim world. Second, the Crusades resulted in increased trade between Europe and the Middle East. The Crusaders developed a taste for perfumes, silks, spices, jewelry, and fruits that they had never seen before. Third, the Crusades increased the pace of economic change that was already being felt in Europe. For example, banks had to be invented to supply Crusaders with credit so that they didn't have to carry money. Finally, the Crusades encouraged Europeans to develop new kinds of ships and **navigation** to carry Crusaders to the Holy Land. Eventually, this knowledge would enable Europeans to explore the coasts of Africa, Asia, and the Americas.

Saladin Accepting the Surrender of the Crusaders After the Muslim Victory in 1187.

Egypt and the Middle East   Crusaders Descend Upon the Middle East

Name: _____   Date: _____

Knowledge Check

Matching

_____ 1. pilgrimage   a. to be taken across a body of water by boat
_____ 2. infidel   b. a European nobleman
_____ 3. pagan   c. a large, heavy, wooden beam used to beat down the wall or
_____ 4. ferried   gate of a city being attacked
_____ 5. count   d. a kingdom
_____ 6. conquer   e. a journey for religious purposes
_____ 7. realm   f. the name Christians called all Muslims
_____ 8. battering ram   g. a person holding religious beliefs other than those of the main
                               religion
                            h. to defeat by force

Multiple Choice

9. Who recaptured Jerusalem from the Crusaders?
   a. Urban II   b. Saladin
   c. Godfrey of Bouillon   d. Alexius Comnenus I

10. On which Crusade did the Europeans capture Constantinople?
    a. The First Crusade   b. The Third Crusade
    c. The Second Crusade   d. The Fourth Crusade

11. Who was the Byzantine emperor who asked for aid from the pope?
    a. Alexius Comnenus I   b. Godfrey of Bouillon
    c. Urban II   d. Saladin

Critical Thinking

12. How do you think the Crusades affected the people of the Middle East? Explain your answer.

_____
_____
_____
_____
_____
_____
_____

The Middle East Under the Power of the Turks

The Ottoman Empire

Osman I

After the Middle Easterners had successfully fought off the Crusaders, they faced a more fearsome enemy: the **Mongols**. These ferocious warriors mounted on sturdy horses rode into the **Middle East** after conquering China. They swept all before them and burned and looted great Islamic cities like Baghdad. Yet, their domination was short-lived. Osman, a prince of a small Turkish principality in the 15th century, gradually carved out for himself a new empire from the remnant of the old.

This new empire was known as the **Ottoman Empire**. With amazing speed, his successors spread the empire in all directions. After Turkey, they conquered the Serbians, then captured Constantinople, bringing the Byzantine Empire to an end. Finally, they captured all of the Middle East and North Africa.

When the Ottomans captured Constantinople, they changed the name of the city to Istanbul. Suleiman the Magnificent was the greatest of the Ottoman rulers. He ruled over a well-run empire from his capital in Istanbul.

A Janissary

For the first 200 years, the Ottoman Empire was ruled by able **sultans**. These men could count also on the loyalty of the slaves collected by the system of **devshirme**. This system was a tax paid to the sultans. Instead of money, the people were required to give young boys to the sultan as slaves. The slaves were trained and later became administrators, **scribes**, and soldiers for the empire. One group of these slaves was the **Janissaries**. They were well-educated in special schools. These slaves made up an elite corps of **infantry**. The Janissaries were kept in closed barracks. They spent their time in endless military drill. They were only allowed out to fight the sultan's enemies.

Decline of the Ottoman Empire

Ottoman Artist

However, even in Suleiman's day, the empire began to show signs of weakness. The Ottomans fell behind the Europeans in technology. While the Europeans developed new and faster sailing ships, the Ottomans still used oar-driven galleys. Conservative religious leaders repressed the use of printing presses so that books were rare. In time, even the Janissaries were no match for European armies with better firearms. Meanwhile, European discoverers found new sea-born trade routes around the coast of Africa to the Far East and across the Atlantic to the New World. Sea travel was much cheaper than carrying goods by land across the Middle East. As a result, **commerce** and trade in the Ottoman Empire deteriorated.

Corruption, too, had weakened the sultan's ability to rule. With the death of Suleiman, the line of strong sultans came to an end. As the world entered the 19th century, the Middle East found itself running desperately behind Europe.

Egypt and the Middle East

The Middle East Under the Power of the Turks

Name: _____ Date: _____

Knowledge Check

Matching

_____ 1. Middle East
_____ 2. Janissaries
_____ 3. commerce
_____ 4. scribes
_____ 5. sultans
_____ 6. Ottoman Empire
_____ 7. infantry

a. the supreme rulers of the Ottoman Empire
b. a soldier trained and equipped to fight on foot
c. the professional writers who kept records and copied letters and official documents for the ruler
d. a region of southwestern Asia and North Africa that stretches from Tunisia to Afghanistan
e. specially trained warrior-slaves
f. the exchange or buying and selling of commodities on a large scale
g. a former Turkish empire that was founded about 1300 by Osman and reached its greatest territorial extent under Suleiman in the 16th century

Multiple Choice

8. After the Crusades were over, who invaded the Middle East?
   a. The Turks
   b. The Greeks
   c. The Seljuk Turks
   d. The Mongols

9. What was the new name of Constantinople?
   a. Turkey
   b. China
   c. Istanbul
   d. Ottoman Empire

10. Who founded the Ottoman Empire?
    a. Ottoman
    b. Osman
    c. Selim
    d. Suleiman

Constructed Response

11. Explain what caused the Ottoman Empire to decline. Use two details from the selection to support your answer.

_____
_____
_____
_____
_____
_____

Egypt and the Middle East

The Middle East Under the Power of the Turks

Name: _____ Date: _____

Map Follow-Up: The Ottoman Empire

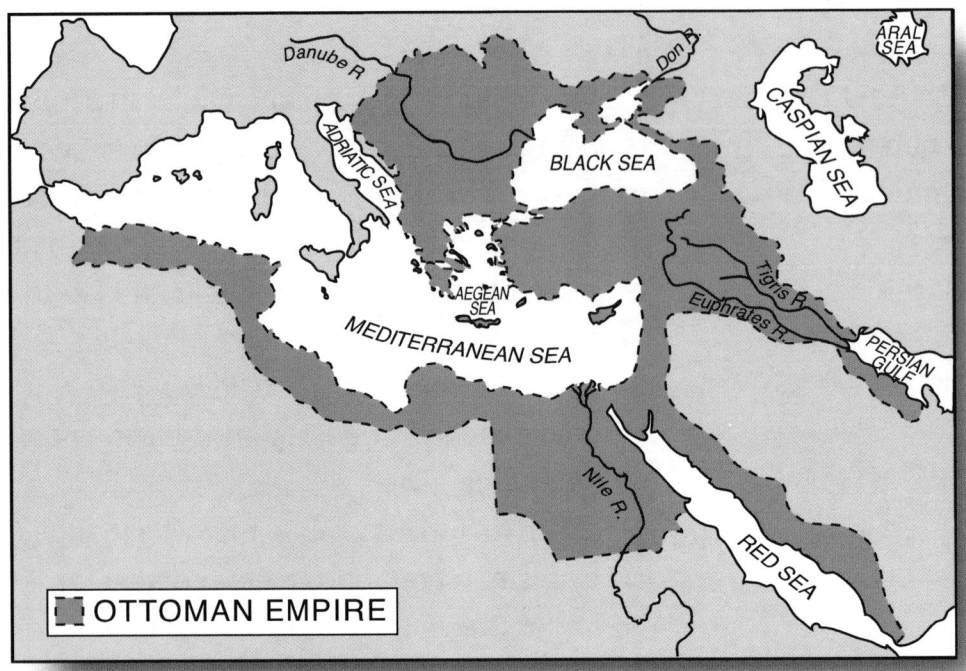

The Ottoman Empire was one of the largest and longest lasting empires in history. At the height of its power, in the 16th and 17th centuries, it controlled territory in southeast Europe, western Asia, and North Africa.

True or False
Circle "T" for True or "F" for False
1. T F The Ottoman Empire was located on the Mediterranean Sea.
2. T F The present day country of Italy was once part of the Ottoman Empire.
3. T F Most of Southern Africa was part of the Ottoman Empire.
4. T F The Ottoman Empire was one of the largest empires in history.
5. T F The Atlantic Ocean was an important waterway for the Ottoman Empire.

Critical Thinking
6. Why do you think the Mediterranean Sea was important to the Ottoman Empire? Explain your answer.

_____
_____
_____
_____
_____

New Forces for Change in the Ottoman Empire

Napoleon Invades Egypt

In the final years of the 18th and the beginning of the 19th century, the Ottoman Empire became a battleground. Russia sought to acquire Ottoman territory along its frontier. France, too, sent Napoleon Bonaparte to invade Egypt. The invasion failed, but it had profound effects. Napoleon brought with him scholars who began to study the ancient remains of Egypt for the first time. They also found the **Rosetta Stone**, which enabled them to **decipher** Egyptian **hieroglyphics**.

The Rosetta Stone had writing in Egyptian hieroglyphs (top), Demotic Egyptian (middle), and Greek (bottom).

For the people of the Middle East, Napoleon's invasion impressed upon them the superior technological capabilities of a European power. The ease with which Napoleon's troops defeated the Egyptian army in the heart of the Middle East was a great shock. After Napoleon was driven out with British help, Middle Easterners redoubled their pleas for reform and modernization.

Reforming the Middle East

Despairing that the Ottomans would never improve the system, Muhammad Ali, the governor of Egypt, declared Egypt independent. He began a program of modernization along European lines. He published the first Arab-language newspaper in 1828. Soon, other Arabic-language newspapers were springing up in Syria, Palestine, and Lebanon. Such developments helped to foster a growing sense of nationalism among the people of the Middle East. **Nationalism** is the belief that a particular group of people sharing the same language and culture should form an independent state.

Around the same time, Greece rebelled and eventually broke free from the Ottoman yoke. This was only the beginning. Nationalism also became popular in the Balkans. In time, the Ottomans lost most of their European possessions. The European powers sometimes even fought over control of Ottoman territory. During the **Crimean War** from 1853 to 1856, Russia fought Britain, France, and Sardinia for possession of Ottoman territories around the Black Sea.

Young Turk Revolutionaries Entering Istanbul

The Egyptians completed the **Suez Canal** in 1869. This created a waterway for ships between the Mediterranean and the Red Sea. The Egyptians had to borrow huge amounts of money from the French and British to complete it. In 1882, Britain used Egypt's inability to pay off its debts as an excuse to invade and occupy Egypt for the next 60 years.

The humiliations suffered by the Ottomans finally persuaded men in power to seek dramatic reforms. A program of reforms was launched called the **Tanzimat**. In 1908, a group of reformers called the **Young Turks** rebelled against the sultan. He was replaced by his more cooperative brother, Mehmet V, and a new government formed under the control of the Young Turks. Although facing enormous problems, they were determined to bring what was left of the Ottoman Empire into the 20th century.

Egypt and the Middle East — New Forces for Change in the Ottoman Empire

Name: _____ Date: _____

Knowledge Check

Matching

_____ 1. Rosetta Stone
_____ 2. nationalism
_____ 3. hieroglyphics
_____ 4. Crimean War
_____ 5. decipher
_____ 6. Suez Canal
_____ 7. Tanzimat

a. a canal connecting the Mediterranean and Red Seas
b. the period of reforms under the Ottoman Empire
c. a black basalt stone found in 1799 that bears an inscription in hieroglyphics, Demotic characters, and Greek that allowed scholars to understand hieroglyphics for the first time
d. the belief that a particular group of people sharing the same language and culture should form an independent state
e. to read or interpret
f. the ancient Egyptian system of picture writing
g. a war from 1853 to 1856 fought over the possession of Ottoman territories around the Black Sea

Multiple Choice

8. What group of reformers rebelled against the sultan in 1908?
   a. the Young Turks
   b. the Nationalists
   c. the Greeks
   d. the Ottomans

9. Who completed the Suez Canal in 1869?
   a. the Greeks
   b. the Egyptians
   c. the Balkans
   d. the Young Turks

10. Who published the first Arab-language newspaper in 1828?
    a. Napoleon
    b. Muhammad Ali
    c. the Young Turks
    d. Mehmet V

Suez Canal

Constructed Response

11. Explain what resulted from Napoleon's invasion of Egypt. Use details from the selection to support your answer.

_____
_____
_____
_____
_____
_____

World War I and the Middle East

A bullet was fired at Sarajevo, Bosnia, on June 28, 1914, and Austrian Archduke Franz Ferdinand slumped over dead. No one could have imagined that this event would lead to a war of such proportions that it would eventually be called **World War I**. For the Middle East, it was the beginning of a new era.

The Oriental Railroad

As was true in parts of Africa, the European powers had struggled for influence in the Middle East for many years. A German company received permission to build a railroad in Turkey from the Bosporus to Ankara; the next year, it got control of the Oriental railroad connecting Austria with Constantinople. Germany wanted to extend the railroad to Baghdad, but Prime Minister Bismarck feared that would cause problems with Russia. The German king, the **Kaiser**, ignored Bismarck's concerns, and in 1898, he persuaded Turkey to allow a railroad to be built to Baghdad. Russia and England both opposed it. Russia feared Germany might block their entrance to the Black Sea. England thought it threatened their interests in Persia and India. The British offered protection to the **sheik** of Kuwait, who promised to make no deals without British approval.

Allied troops from Australia and New Zealand landed at ANZAC Cove for the invasion of the Gallipoli Peninsula on April 25, 1915.

Turkey and Germany Become Allies

Turkey was ruled by an incompetent council, held power over its Christian and Arab subjects by brutal force, and stank with corruption. The **Young Turks**, long critical of their predecessors, were no more able to reform the Ottoman Empire than those they had replaced. The real leaders, Talaat Pasha and War Minister Enver Pasha, did not realize the risks they were taking in foreign policy. They were eager to get into Europe's war on Germany's side, thinking that with the Kaiser's help they could seize land in the Caucasus region from Russia. In August 1914, they signed a secret **alliance** with Germany and waited until October to announce it. By getting involved, they were going to cross England, Russia, and France.

When World War I began, Turkey was brutally expelling Greeks from their soil, and tension was growing with Greece. The United States sold Greece two old battleships that were better than any ships in the Turkish navy. The Turks had paid the British to build two battleships for them, but they had not been delivered before the war began. Lord of the Admiralty, Winston Churchill decided not to send the ships because England needed them; he did not know that Turkey had already signed on the enemy side. Two German cruisers sailed to Turkey, where they flew the Turkish flag, but the captains and crews were Germans. These ships were able to keep the Russians from breaking through the **Bosporus** to the Mediterranean. Russia asked England for help, and England was eager to get involved.

Britain Invades Gallipoli Peninsula

The British navy was converting to ships powered by oil and needed to keep Middle-Eastern oil fields in friendly hands. Churchill pushed hard for an invasion of the Gallipoli Peninsula; if successful, they could attack Constantinople. An English army was raised for the attack, and the soldiers were thrilled by the opportunity; "Gallipoli fever" spread through the confident men. The Turks, trained by the Germans, were also eager for a fight. Their leader, General Mustafa Kemal, told them: "I don't order you to attack; I order you to die." The invaders suffered 20,000 casualties, and the attack stalled. Public reaction in Great Britian grew so angry that the prime minister fired Churchill. A new attack was planned and carried out, but eventually the British, Australian, and New Zealand troops were withdrawn.

Turkish General Mustafa Kemal and His Officers

Lawrence of Arabia

Thomas E. Lawrence was more successful. A scholar, he had traveled through Syria on foot while studying Crusader architecture. He knew the language, culture, and people. When World War I broke out, he was sent to Egypt, where he began organizing the **Arab Bureau**. His purpose was to organize Arabs unhappy under Turkish rule. He made friends with **Emir** (Prince) Faisal, and persuaded him to help drive the Turks from Arab soil. With the support of General Edmund Allenby, his **guerilla warfare** nearly cut the railroad to Damascus. In a war short on heroes, he was known as "Lawrence of Arabia." The Arabs had supported the British and expected the British to be on their side after the war. Lawrence would later criticize Britain for not protecting the Arab interests better.

Emir Faisal (front) led the Arab delegation to the Paris Peace Conference of 1919. T.E. Lawrence is in the second row, second from right.

World War I Ends

After war began between Britain and Turkey in November 1914, a British-Indian army was sent to Iraq, and it captured the Turkish fort at Fao (southern tip of Iraq). The purpose of the expedition was to keep the oil fields from enemy use, keep the Germans from using Basra as a submarine base, and protect India from German attack. In 1917, the British captured Baghdad. When Russia withdrew from the war and pulled their troops out of northeastern Iraq, the British moved northward, taking Kirkuk in May 1918. As the war was coming to an end, the British were near Mosul (northwestern Iraq). After Turkey surrendered, the British took Mosul. Persia (Iran) was barely independent, with Russia willing and able to force its will on its southern neighbor. England and France had agreed in 1907 to divide influence there, with Russia strong in northern Persia. When the Persians tried to take control of their own affairs, the Russian army marched into Tehran. With Germany as a threat, the British ignored terrible crimes committed by Russian troops against Iranians.

When the war ended with German surrender, the fates of Germany, Austria-Hungary, and Turkey were going to be decided by the victors. Whatever they decided was going to have a major effect on the Middle East.

Egypt and the Middle East
World War I and the Middle East

Name: _____ Date: _____

Knowledge Check

Matching

_____ 1. alliance
_____ 2. Kaiser
_____ 3. Bosporus
_____ 4. Young Turks
_____ 5. sheik
_____ 6. guerilla warfare
_____ 7. emir

a. irregular attacks by small units harrassing and sabotaging the enemy
b. an Arab leader
c. the members of a Turkish reform group
d. a narrow strait of water connecting the Black Sea and the Mediterranean Sea
e. the German king
f. an agreement between countries to work together in war or trade
g. a prince in an Islamic country

Multiple Choice

8. Who organized the Arab Bureau?
   a. T. E. Lawrence
   b. Winston Churchill
   c. Talaat Pasha
   d. Enver Pasha

9. This person's death in 1914 led to World War I.
   a. General Mustafa Kemal
   b. Emir Faisal
   c. Archduke Franz Ferdinand
   d. Winston Churchill

10. Which group of people captured Baghdad in 1917?
    a. Germans
    b. British
    c. Persians
    d. Australians

Constructed Response

11. Explain why the Turkish policy of supporting Germany was risky. Use details from the selection to support your answer.

_____
_____
_____
_____
_____
_____
_____

The Mandate System

Three men sat around a table in Versailles, France, discussing the future of the world. We have all thought about how we would improve the world if we could, but their conversations were different. Those three men had the power to decide how millions of people in Europe, Asia, Africa, and the Middle East were going to be ruled in the years ahead.

British Prime Minister David Lloyd George, Italian Premier Vittorio Orlando, French Premier Georges Clemenceau, and American President Woodrow Wilson at the Paris Peace Conference in 1919

President Wilson's Fourteen Points

The idealist, U.S. President Woodrow Wilson, thought war was a terrible thing, and he was determined that **World War I** was going to be the last of its kind. When the United States entered World War I in 1917, he said: "The world must be made safe for democracy." To make that happen, he proposed his famous **Fourteen Points** to bring about world peace.

Three of the Points were especially important to the Middle East. Point 5 said that **colonial** claims must be considered with equal weight given to the interests of the people affected and to the government that would rule them. Point 12 said that Turkey should be independent, and other peoples ruled by Turkey should have self-rule. Point 14 called for "a general association of nations" (this became the **League of Nations**) to guarantee independence to great and small nations alike.

Prime Minister David Lloyd George of Great Britain wanted to take control of German colonies around the world. Premier Georges Clemenceau of France was less interested in colonies than in punishing Germany by taking some of its land and making it pay the cost of the war.

The conference decided German colonies could not be made free but were to become **mandates** of "advanced nations." Each year, progress being made in the Middle East would be reported to the League of Nations. All of the mandates in the Middle East were given to England and France, and the desires of the people for independence were ignored.

Middle East from 1920 to 1939

TURKEY went through major changes. Mustafa Kemal replaced the sultan in 1922 and ruled as president of Turkey and president-general of the National People's Party. In 1935, he took the surname Ataturk. The legislature was no problem for him—he chose all its members himself. Under his rule, **polygamy** ended. Women no longer had to wear veils and were allowed to go to school. Highways and railroads were built, and industry expanded.

SYRIA and LEBANON were French mandates. The French had trouble controlling Syria

Circassian (or Adyghe) Troops in Damascus Under the Command of a French Officer During the Time of the French Mandate

because French officials were high-handed and the people were determined to be free. In 1925, French tanks rolled against rebels in Damascus, killing about 1,000 people. Syria was allowed to write a constitution in 1930 that permitted France to control Syria's foreign policy. It was not until 1945 that Syria received its freedom. Lebanon was different from other Middle Eastern countries. It had a large Christian population, and even the Turks had allowed them freedom in economic matters. In 1941, Lebanon received full independence.

TRANSJORDAN, the region east of Palestine, was a British mandate until 1946 ruled by King Abdullah. This mandate ran smoothly.

IRAQ was also a British mandate ruled by Emir Faisal, the brother of Transjordan's king. Much progress was made in Iraq: a parliament was set up, transportation and communications greatly improved, and its oil resources were developed. By 1936, it was the eighth-leading oil producer in the world. There were serious problems, however. The people strongly resented British rule. Relations with Turkey were poor, and they argued over where to draw the boundary. In 1932 Iraq was given its independence. After Emir Faisal's death in 1933, the nation was troubled by riots, a massacre of hundreds of Christians by Iraqi troops, and efforts to topple the government. The Germans and Italians used the confusion in Iraq to advantage, adding to British concerns about how to handle Iraq.

IRAN was still independent, but its fabulous oil wealth was controlled by the British-owned Anglo-Iranian Oil Company. In 1925, Reza Khan came to power as **Shah** and modernized the nation. He replaced religious courts with regular courts. He expanded education and created the first university in the country in 1934. He increased the number of roads from 2,000 miles to 15,000 miles and built the 1,000-mile-long Trans-Iranian Railway. In 1937, the shah gave American companies the right to develop oil fields in eastern Iran. A few Iranians got rich, but most were as poor as ever.

Construction of the Trans-Iranian Railray

ARABIA had many warring tribes. The most important leader of that desert region was Ibn Saud, an imposing and able leader who took the warring tribes of the desert and built them into a nation. Between the wars, the only important trade came from tourists going to the Muslim holy cities. Oil fields were just beginning to be developed, and in 1936, Saudi Arabia produced only 1.25 million barrels. The first automobile reached Saudi Arabia in 1926, and in 1930, there were still only 1,500 cars in the country.

EGYPT had its own king, but the British military controlled the country. In 1936, British troops left Cairo, but 10,000 troops and 400 planes remained to protect the Suez Canal.

Throughout the Middle East, Western influence was growing, with Great Britain, France, and the United States increasingly involved in the affairs of the region. More **progressive** people of the region saw the need to modernize, but **conservatives** feared that traditions were in danger of being lost forever.

Egypt and the Middle East — The Mandate System

Name: _____ Date: _____

Knowledge Check

Matching

____ 1. polygamy
____ 2. mandate
____ 3. League of Nations
____ 4. shah
____ 5. Fourteen Points
____ 6. progressive
____ 7. World War I
____ 8. conservative

a. the authority to control the Middle-Eastern countries after World War I
b. interested in maintaining existing views, conditions, or institutions; traditional
c. the practice of having more than one wife at one time
d. a peace program proposed by President Woodrow Wilson
e. an international organization created in 1919 by the Allied Powers to try to prevent future wars
f. the Persian word for emperor
g. interested in new ideas and opportunities; moving forward
h. a war fought from 1914 to 1918

Multiple Choice

9. Which leader seemed most interested in inheriting German colonies?
   a. Woodrow Wilson
   b. David Lloyd George
   c. Mustafa Kemal Ataturk
   d. Emir Faisal

10. What area of Syrian life did the French control after 1930?
    a. schools
    b. highways and railroads
    c. homeland security
    d. foreign policy

11. What year did Lebanon finally receive full independence?
    a. 1925
    b. 1930
    c. 1941
    d. 1946

Constructed Response

12. Explain the progress made in Iraq when it was ruled by Emir Faisal. Use at least two details from the selection to support your answer.

_____
_____
_____
_____
_____
_____

The Middle East and World War II

Middle-Eastern Oil

As the nations of Europe and Asia moved closer to war in the 1930s, the Middle East became important again. Middle-Eastern oil could be a big factor in deciding which side won the war. Also vital was the need for a supply line to Russia, which could best be reached by a route through Iran.

Turkey had learned its lesson in World War I and had no intention of getting involved. When Germany's westward advance was stopped at the English Channel, Hitler's need for oil caused him to develop a bold but risky policy that involved the Middle East. Germany would go around Turkey. One army was to drive into Russia, and after punching its way through the Caucasus Mountains and Georgia, it could reach the oil fields from the north. The other army was to attack Egypt, and after reaching the Suez Canal, nothing could stop it from reaching the oil fields from the south.

Part of the Panzer Division of the Afrika Korps on the Move in North Africa in 1942

At first, it looked like the plan was working. In 1942 General Erwin Rommel's **Afrika Korps** reached El Alamein, only 70 miles from Cairo. The German advance into Russia succeeded in reaching Stalingrad. That was as far as either army advanced, however.

Important Areas of the Middle East

Four areas of the Middle East were especially important to the United States and Great Britain after the war ended.

IRAQ was ruled by a three-year-old king when World War II began in 1939. The most powerful leader in the country was Nuri al-Sa'id. Nuri was too pro-British to suit many officers in the army, who admired the success of the Germans. A group known as the "**Four Colonels**" overthrew Nuri in 1941 and made Rashid Ali the premier. Within a month, the British began working to overthrow Rashid. With a small army marching out of Transjordan, they defeated a much larger Iraqi army, and Rashid was forced into exile. Nuri returned to power, and the government declared war on Germany in 1943. The Four Colonels remained heroes in the minds of many Iraqis, however, because they tried to free the country from British influence.

Saudi Arabian King Ibn Saud and American President Franklin D. Roosevelt talk while on a ship returning from a war conference in 1945.

SAUDI ARABIA was officially **neutral** in the war until 1945, but from the beginning, it favored England. During the war, the flow of tourists to Mecca and Medina dropped drastically, and the nation was in a terrible financial slump. Great Britain and the United States gave them money to keep the country running. The United States had four good reasons to help the Saudis: (1) growing concern over the amount of oil being pumped from American fields, (2) future interests of the **Arabian-American Oil Company** (ARAMCO), (3) the desire to keep military bases on Arabian soil, and (4) to keep the friendship of the king.

IRAN had the best route for sending aid to Russia. The United States and Great Britain joined Russia in interfering in Iranian affairs. The **Tudeh Party** was an Iranian version of the Communist Party and was very active. To counter Russian influence in northern Iran, the British moved troops into southern Iran. The British and Russians agreed that their troops were to leave Iran six months after the war ended. The United States also sent a few troops and advisers to help Iran handle its finances and internal security.

PALESTINE was the home Jews around the world dreamed one day would be theirs again. That idea was strengthened when Russia's **czars** began **pogroms**, government-approved attacks on Jewish people and property. These caused millions of Jews to go to the United States, but others planned for a return to Palestine. Leaders like Leo Pinsker and Theodor Herzl saw the need for a Jewish nation in the 19th century.

In 1917, the British cabinet approved the **Balfour Declaration**: "His Majesty's Government view with favour the establishment in Palestine of a National Home for the Jewish people and will use their best endeavors to facilitate the achievement of this objective, it being clearly understood that nothing shall be done which may prejudice the civil and religious rights of existing non-Jewish communities in Palestine." This was very vague, and how it could be achieved was a mystery.

Jews began moving to Palestine after World War I, buying land from absentee landlords. The number of Jews in Palestine was 174,000 in 1931, but that rose to 382,000 by 1936. Palestinian Arabs, feeling threatened by their lack of influence with the British government and by the growing number of Jewish settlers, rioted in 1936, and the British agreed to limit Jewish immigration. In 1937, the **Peel Commission** was sent to Palestine; it recommended that Palestine be divided into one nation for Jews and another for Arabs. Jewish leaders, however, thought the amount of land allowed them by the plan was too small, and they opposed it.

Other Arabs were growing concerned about Palestine, and Great Britain knew they would need Arab oil in case of a war with Germany. So British leaders issued the "**White Paper**" of 1939, saying that it was not their policy that Palestine should become a Jewish State. During World War II, **Zionist** groups inside Palestine pressured Britain to leave by attacking British troops. Terror organizations like the **Irgun**, led by Menachem Begin, and the **Lehi** (Stern Group) also made occasional attacks.

This Irgun poster from 1931 promotes establishing an Israeli homeland.

During **World War II**, over six million Jews were killed by the German Nazis. Villages were wiped out, and Jews were taken to **concentration camps** where they were killed or held prisoner in horrible conditions. This led public pressure in the United States and Britain to turn toward ending the mandate and creating a Jewish state. In 1947, the United Nations approved the new State of Israel, and on May 14, 1948, it was born.

Egypt and the Middle East

The Middle East and World War II

Name: _____ Date: _____

Knowledge Check

Matching

____ 1. neutral
____ 2. czars
____ 3. Zionist
____ 4. Balfour Declaration
____ 5. pogrom
____ 6. Afrika Korps
____ 7. Lehi

a. government-approved attacks on Jewish people and property in Russia
b. a German army force sent to North Africa in 1941 under General Rommel
c. a Zionist terrorist group also called the Stern Group
d. the position of not taking sides in a war or conflict
e. a statement issued by the British government favoring setting up a national home for the Jews in Palestine
f. a king or emperor of Russia
g. a Jewish movement for the development and protection of a Jewish nation in Israel

Multiple Choice

8. What oil company operated in Saudi Arabia?
   a. British-Italian Oil Company
   b. Arabian-American Oil Company
   c. Spanish-American Oil Company
   d. German-Italian Oil Company

9. What was the Iranian version of the Communist Party called?
   a. the Tudeh Party
   b. the Zionist Party
   c. the White Paper Party
   d. the Four Colonels Party

10. What was the Irgun organization?
    a. church organization
    b. political organization
    c. terror organization
    d. civil rights organization

11. Where were Jews taken to be killed or held prisoner during World War II?
    a. mandates
    b. villages
    c. Palestine
    d. concentration camps

Critical Thinking

12. Why do you think the Middle East continues to play an important part in wars and conflicts? Use information you have learned throughout this book to help support your answer.

_____
_____
_____
_____
_____

Israel

Israel Becomes a Nation

A tough and determined new nation was founded in the Middle East in 1948. It was going to have to fight in order to survive there. Israelis knew what they were up against, and they moved quickly to prepare for the struggle.

The Jewish underground army in Palestine, the **Haganah**, had armed itself with modern weapons from Europe. Its officers were well trained, and many had combat experience. There were no illusions about an easy start; Arab nations left no doubt that they were determined to wipe Israel off the face of the earth.

Trouble began May 15, 1948, the day after Israel was officially recognized. Five Arab nations, from Egypt to Iraq, contributed troops to attacks on Israel. However, these attacks were poorly planned, and within a year, all the nations agreed to an **armistice** with Israel. During that war, many Arabs left Israel, but no Arab nation wanted them.

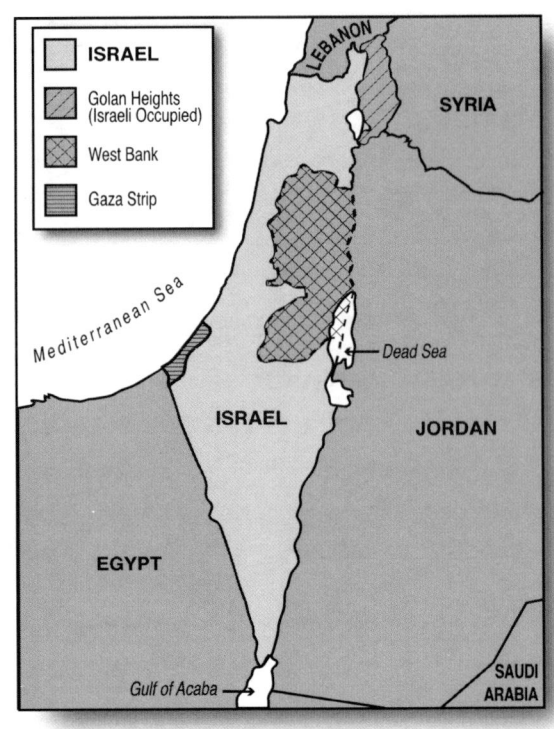

They ended up in camps behind barbed wire. By 1949, the Arab population of Israel had dropped from the 1.3 million it had been in 1946 to only 160,000. Those who had lost their homes or who were born in the camps that were set up had bitter feelings against Israel and the United States, whom they blamed for creating Israel. Between 1948 and January 1, 1956, 771,000 Jews moved to Israel.

The government of Israel was democratic. From 1949 to 1963, the **prime minister** was David Ben-Gurion. The legislature, the **Knesset**, included members from many different parties, the largest being the **Mapai**. Since it did not have a majority, the Mapai was forced to make deals with the smaller parties to get anything done.

Surrounded by enemy nations, Israel built up its military strength. Men served three years in the army and then served in the reserves. Unmarried women served 20 months and then entered the reserves. The Israeli navy in 1968 included two destroyers and four submarines. Their air force had 350 of the most advanced planes available and some of the best pilots in the world.

Aswan High Dam on the Nile River in Egypt

Nations Surrounding Israel

EGYPT was ruled by Gamal Abd al-Nasser after 1954. Nasser had ideas about making his nation stronger. His grand dream was to build the **Aswan Dam** on the Nile River to increase Egypt's electrical output and prevent the annual floods. The United States and Great Britain agreed to pay for the first studies, but Nasser hinted that he might see if the Russians would give him a better deal. The United States and Britain withdrew their offer to help. Nasser then angrily threatened to seize the Suez Canal from its British and French stockholders. Israel attacked Egypt on October 29, and British and

French **paratroops** landed near the canal on October 31, 1956. Russia, seeing the opportunity to win friends with the Arabs, threatened to send "volunteers" to help Egypt. President Eisenhower used U.S. influence against its allies in the United Nations, and a **cease-fire** was arranged.

SYRIA was a divided nation. It was an Islamic nation, but it had a large Christian minority. Some Syrians looked to Egypt for leadership, and others preferred Iraqi leadership. Some wanted modern lifestyles while others favored traditional Arab lifestyles. The largest Syrian political party was the **Ba'ath** [Ba-kth], and it favored Arab unity. In 1957, the Ba'ath Party asked Nasser from Egypt to unite the two countries. They joined in 1958 as the **United Arab Republic** (UAR). The union did not work, and in 1961 the UAR broke up.

Egypt's Gamal Abd al-Nasser (front row, fourth from left) with Syrian and Egyptian Cabinet Members of the United Arab Republic in 1958

IRAQ was still a nation with only a few wealthy landowners and a vast majority of people who were very poor. In 1958, a **coup** (rebellion inside a government) led by Colonel Qasim took the lives of the king and his advisors. This was the beginning of a constant struggle for power, as one ruler after another was overthrown. Adding to tension was the desire of Iraqi **Kurds** to unite with other Kurds in Iran and Turkey to form their own nation. Meanwhile, Iraq's foreign policy turned away from Britain and the United States toward Russia.

JORDAN, east of Israel, was now home to thousands of Palestinian **refugees**. In 1953, King Hussein became ruler of that troubled land. There were many attempts to kill him or overthrow his government, but he held firm with the help of his army. Inside Egypt, Syria, Iraq, and Jordan was one unifying thought: to destroy the State of Israel.

The Six-Day War (War of 1967)

The Six-Day War involved Israel and its neighboring countries. In 1966, Syria began picking fights with Israel, and Israel responded with air raids. Egypt agreed to help Syria, and Nasser closed the Suez Canal to Israeli ships. Jordan joined the other Arabs. In a war lasting only six days, from June 5 to 10, 1967, Israel captured the entire Sinai desert to the east bank of the Suez Canal, Jordan's territory west of the Jordan River (the **West Bank**), and the **Golan Heights** from Syria. Israel offered to trade the captured land for peace treaties, but the defeated neighbors refused.

The **Palestine Liberation Organization (PLO)** was an outgrowth of this war. In 1969, it chose Yasser Arafat as its leader. So many Palestinians in Jordan joined the PLO that they threatened King Hussein's control of his own nation. In 1970, his troops put down the PLO, which moved its operations to Lebanon instead.

The Yom Kippur War

The Yom Kippur War of 1973 was another war against Israel. Egypt and Syria jointly attacked Israel at the beginning of its **Yom Kippur** religious observance (October 6, 1973) and caught Israel completely off guard. After some territory had been taken, the Israelis regrouped and stormed back. They not only recovered the ground they had lost, but drove the Egyptians beyond the Suez Canal. Now Israel held both banks of the canal.

Egypt and the Middle East   Israel

Name: _____ Date: _____

Knowledge Check

Matching

_____ 1. Mapai
_____ 2. paratroops
_____ 3. prime minister
_____ 4. refugee
_____ 5. cease-fire
_____ 6. coup
_____ 7. Haganah
_____ 8. United Arab Republic
_____ 9. Kurds

a. a rebellion inside a government
b. the head of an elected government
c. the Jewish underground army in Palestine
d. tribe of Islamic people living in Iraq, Iran, and Turkey
e. a temporary suspension of fighting
f. the largest political party in Israel's early years
g. a person who has been forced to leave a country in order to escape war, persecution, or natural disaster
h. soldiers trained and equipped to parachute from an airplane
i. the union of Egypt and Syria from 1958 to 1961

Multiple Choice

10. Who was the leader of Israel from 1949 to 1963?
    a. David Ben-Gurion
    b. Colonel Qasim
    c. Yasser Arafat
    d. Gamal Abd al-Nasser

11. What is the name of Israel's legislature?
    a. Knesset
    b. PLO
    c. United Arab Republic
    d. Haganah

12. Who wanted the Aswan Dam for electricity and flood control?
    a. Colonel Qasim
    b. David Ben-Gurion
    c. President Eisenhower
    d. Gamal Abd al-Nasser

Constructed Response

13. Explain the result of the Yom Kippur War of 1973. Use details from the selection to support your answer.

_____
_____
_____
_____
_____
_____
_____

Oil Brings Changes to the Middle East

Rising Oil Prices

Generations in every country share different experiences. Your grandparents lived through times that seem like ancient history to you. But think of the changes that occurred between 1940 and 1980 in the Middle East. The grandfather's camel was replaced by the grandson's car. The grandfather was uneducated, while his grandson had a college degree. Grandfather had fought his wars with a sword. The grandson piloted a jet fighter. The world ignored the grandfather, but it paid close attention to the grandson. The difference between the generations was the power of oil.

The OPEC Flag

In 1960, a trade organization called the **Organization of Petroleum Exporting Countries (OPEC)** was formed by Iran, Iraq, Kuwait, Saudi Arabia, and Venezuela. By 1973, OPEC had grown to 13 members interested in raising oil prices. Oil was not only improving the Middle East's standard of living, but it was building the fast-growing economies of Japan, Europe, and the United States. Gasoline was cheap, which inspired manufacturers to build cars getting only 12 to 15 miles per gallon. Home insulation wasn't needed when fuel oil sold at 12 cents a gallon. Wasted energy resources could not be replaced, however, and sooner or later, producer and consumer were going to pay for the extravagance.

Rising gas prices led to the Energy Crisis of 1973.

On January 1, 1973, oil sold for $2.74 a **barrel** (55 gallons); a year later, it sold for $11.65. This 400-percent increase was due to Arab reaction to the 1973 war between Israel and its neighbors. When the war began, President Nixon sent $2.2 billion worth of military aid to Israel. Saudi Arabia responded by cutting all oil shipments to the United States and Europe. OPEC announced it was reducing oil production. Lines formed at gas pumps in the United States, and consumers used to paying 26 cents a gallon now paid 40 to 50 cents. This price increase sent shock waves through the economies of Asia, Europe, and the United States. The United States had its own oil resources, but many countries were completely dependent on Arab oil. When OPEC met, the powerful nations held their breath.

Wealth and Influence Affect the Region

SAUDI ARABIA, still in many ways a traditional Arab nation, stood at the top of the class for **oil reserves**, with Iran third, Kuwait fourth, and other Persian Gulf nations fifth. The only outside nation in the top five was Russia, and the United States ranked seventh. To the common people of Saudi Arabia, life went on pretty much as before: prayer five times a day, women wearing long black veils, and no theaters or bars. U.S. and other foreign workers lived very comfortably, but they were in communities isolated from the Saudis.

King Faisal Al Saud followed a policy of **modernization** in economic matters. He built sewage and water treatment plants, hospitals, and schools. He paved roads and built a strong air force with the latest planes. The conservative Muslim social order remained. Saudi homes had separate entrances for women, and women were not allowed to drive cars or ride alone in taxis. Punishments were traditional. After three convictions for theft, a hand was cut off; **capital punishment** was by beheading.

The full force of Saudi power could not be used against the United States because so many of the skilled oil workers were American, and the United States was their most powerful friend and protector. In 1979, some military officers attempted a coup against King Khalid that was put down. The Saudis signed an agreement with the United States to guarantee its independence under the present rulers. In return, Saudi Arabia increased oil production.

Israel was less of a threat to the Saudis than Muslim **fanatics** were. In 1979, fanatics seized control of the Grand Mosque at Mecca and held the worshippers hostage until the National Guard captured them. This problem increased when the Ayatollah Khomeini came to power in Iran as its religious leader.

KUWAIT was a small nation squeezed between Saudi Arabia and Iraq on the Persian Gulf. Independent since 1961, its greatest threat to survival was Iraq. Kuwait's oil had more sulphur than was normal, so it did not receive the highest prices. However, with the price of oil jumping in 1973, Kuwait's oil looked more attractive, and it became an important player in the oil business. In 1977, the government took over the foreign oil companies and made them part of the **Kuwait Petroleum Corporation (KPC)**. The increased price of oil made it possible for Kuwait to create a **welfare state** with the government providing medical care, education, and even free drinking water.

IRAN had been ruled since 1941 by Shah Mohammad Reza Pahlavi. During World War II, British and Russian troops were sent there, and when the war ended, the Russians stayed until the United States and Great Britain pressured them to leave. Relations with Britain were bad because many Iranians resented the British-owned Anglo-Iranian Oil Company (AIOC). In 1951, Premier Mohammad Mossadegh nationalized the company against British opposition. In 1953, a coup aided by the United States and Britain overthrew him. A new arrangement followed whereby oil companies shared profits equally with Iran.

The shah's program included land reform and modernizing the country but without political freedom. When the price of oil rose in 1973, he had dreams of making Iran into a great world power, but progress led to high inflation, political protest, and the arrest of critics by **SAVAK** (the secret police). In 1964, he exiled

The Shah of Iran, Mohammad Reza Pahlavi, (right) met with members of OPEC during an OPEC session in Tehran, Iran, in 1970.

the Ayatollah Khomeini, who eventually went to Paris. Mass demonstrations broke out against the shah in January 1979, and this time, nothing could stop them. The shah and his wife left Iran on January 16. Khomeini returned to Iran on February 1, 1979.

Egypt and the Middle East
Oil Brings Changes to the Middle East

Name: _____ Date: _____

Knowledge Check

Matching

_____ 1. barrel
_____ 2. modernization
_____ 3. OPEC
_____ 4. capital punishment
_____ 5. SAVAK
_____ 6. fanatics
_____ 7. welfare state
_____ 8. oil reserves

a. the Iranian secret police
b. a trade organization of oil exporting nations
c. a country where the government pays for medical care, education, and other services
d. the supply of oil that can be brought into production from a nation's oil fields
e. a container holding fifty-five gallons of oil
f. death by execution for committing a crime
g. those who are intensely devoted to a cause
h. to adopt modern ways

Multiple Choice

9. How much did oil cost in January 1973?
   a. $11.65 a barrel
   b. $3.74 a barrel
   c. $2.74 a barrel
   d. $12.65 a barrel

10. How much did oil cost in January 1974?
    a. $12.65 a barrel
    b. $11.65 a barrel
    c. $3.76 a barrel
    d. $2.74 a barrel

11. What nation ranked first in oil reserves in the early 1970s?
    a. Iran
    b. Saudi Arabia
    c. Venezuela
    d. Kuwait

Constructed Response

12. Explain King Faisal Al Saud's policy of modernization in economic matters. Use two details from the selection to support your answer.

_____

_____

_____

_____

_____

_____

Explore: Middle East Travel Brochure

Some of the world's most fascinating ancient sites and luxurious modern resorts are in the Middle East. A travel brochure is a way for nations and businesses to attract more tourists and customers. A well-planned and designed brochure includes things that would be of interest to tourists.

Materials:

Internet
reference books
plain white paper 8 1/2" x 11"
colored markers or pencils
old travel magazines
clip art
glue stick

Directions:

Step 1: Research one of the countries of the Middle East. Use the information to create a tri-fold travel brochure. The brochure might include the following sections:

- brief description of the country
- map identifying the geography, major cities, well-known places, historic sites, and landmarks
- list of recreation and outdoor activities—parks, sports, water, or entertainment
- climate and overall weather conditions
- transportation
- museums and theaters
- languages
- popular food
- shopping centers

Step 2: Fold white paper into thirds.

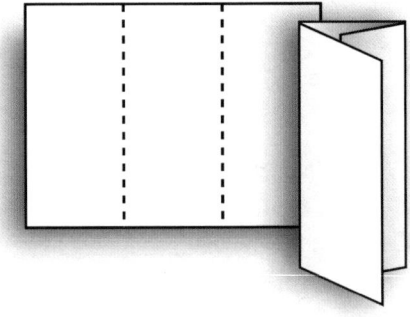

Step 3: Organize the information and pictures from your research on each panel of the tri-fold.

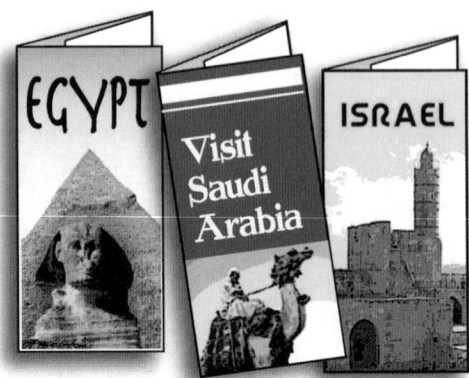

Step 4: Share with classmates.

Khomeini Takes on the United States

Ayatollah Ruhollah Khomeini

Born in 1900, Ruhollah Khomeini was a **Shiite Muslim** with a hatred for the modernism of Islam. A scholar of Islamic teachings, he was honored with the title of **ayatollah** (teacher) in the 1950s. His often-expressed dislike for the **Shah** of Iran led to his imprisonment and in 1964 to his **exile** to Iraq. His further accusations against the Iranian ruler caused Iraq to expel him. In 1978, he and his second wife were exiled to Paris.

Khomeini blamed the United States, which he called the "great Satan," for supporting the corrupt shah and his puppets, who paid no taxes but spent millions on **arms**. The United States appreciated the shah's help in supplying American oil needs, but made the mistake of ignoring the abuses by SAVAK (the Iranian secret police) and the growing rift between the shah and his people. The United States blamed disturbances on a few religious zealots or the Communist Tudeh Party.

The Shah Leaves Iran and Americans Are Taken Hostage

Khomeini sent taped messages into Iran that were broadcast to the country by religious backers. In October 1978, he called for a general strike, and that was followed the next month by strikes of oil field workers. The success of these efforts paralyzed the economy and made it clear that Khomeini had more power among the people than the shah.

The shah was forced to leave Iran in January 1979, and he began drifting from one country to another. Khomeini returned to Iran on February 1, 1979. Also in February, the Tudeh Party captured the U.S. **embassy** and held its personnel hostage. Khomeini ordered that they be freed, and they were set free immediately. Then the shah came to the United States in October for cancer treatment. Khomeini was furious with President Jimmy Carter for allowing the shah to enter the country, and demonstrations outside the U.S. embassy in Tehran began. Again, mobs stormed the embassy, but this time, embassy personnel were captured with Khomeini's permission. Americans at home rallied around the hostages, and yellow ribbons were put around trees as a sign of support. The United States demanded that the embassy personnel be released.

President Jimmy Carter speaks at a state dinner during the Shah of Iran's visit to America in 1977.

Khomeini held no government titles, but it was clear that no Iranian official dared act in any way without his approval. Going through normal **diplomatic** channels did not work, and a frustrated President Jimmy Carter tried a number of approaches in his efforts to get the Americans out. As soon as the shah was healthy enough to travel, he was sent to Panama, where he died in 1980. The United States put an **embargo** on Iranian oil. Then, in April 1980, the United States sent helicopters into Iran to try to rescue the hostages. Two helicopters went down in the Iranian desert during the failed rescue attempt.

Problems in the Region Grow

In the meantime, all kinds of problems were breaking out in the region. The United States got involved in the struggle between rival leaders in Afghanistan when the American **ambassador** was kidnapped and killed. The Russians decided to take charge of the Afghan situation and moved troops in. The United States saw this as a clear sign of Russian **imperialism** and took several actions designed to punish the Soviets, including a grain embargo and refusal to send athletes to the 1980 Olympic Games held in Moscow.

Iran was having its troubles as well. Inside the country, a struggle was going on for control of the government. Supporters of Khomeini formed the **Islamic Republic Party** (IRP), and it got control of the parliament and opposed the elected president, Bani-Sadr. The president lost the support of Khomeini and was impeached. Rising to oppose the IRP was the **Mujahedin**, who backed Massud Rajavi. Both sides used terror, and political murders and arrests became common.

Iran was now unpopular with both the United States and Russia and was torn by internal conflict. Saddam Hussein of Iraq decided this was a good time to push Iran back from oil fields along the border between the two nations. In September 1980 Iraq attacked, and for two years had the upper hand. The Iranians succeeded in taking back most of the lost territory by 1982, but Khomeini kept the war going in the hope of defeating Hussein.

The United States was engaged in a struggle for power as well—one far more peaceful. Carter won the Democratic nomination for a second term, but Ronald Reagan, the Republican challenger, won the 1980 presidential election by a large margin. Part of the reason for Carter's defeat was the failure of his policies toward Iran and Afghanistan. Reagan was no friendlier toward the Iranians than Carter. He called them "nothing better than criminals and kidnappers." Like Carter, he refused to consider paying any **ransom** for the return of the captives.

Both the United States and Iran had good reason to see the issue settled. The last details of an arrangement were worked out in January 1981. As Reagan was being **inaugurated** president on January 20, the Iranians released the hostages. They had been held for 444 days. Both nations had been hurt by the crisis. Iran had been damaged by the war with Iraq and the steps backward under strict Islamic rules. The United States suffered from the rise in the cost of oil and the loss of a stable and friendly government in Iran.

The freed American hostages finally landed in the United States on January 25, 1981.

Egypt and the Middle East | Khomeini Takes on the United States

Name: _____ Date: _____

Knowledge Check

Matching

____ 1. exile
____ 2. imperialism
____ 3. embargo
____ 4. embassy
____ 5. shah
____ 6. ayatollah
____ 7. ambassador
____ 8. Shiite

a. a Shiite religious teacher in Iran
b. a restriction that a government puts on the buying and selling of certain goods
c. the Persian word for emperor
d. an enforced removal from one's native country
e. a person who is sent by a country as its representative to a foreign country
f. a Muslim of the Shia branch of Islam
g. a policy of extending a country's power and influence over other countries through diplomacy or military force
h. the official residence of an ambassador

Multiple Choice

9. Why did President Carter allow the shah to enter the United States?
   a. For gall bladder surgery
   b. For cancer treatments
   c. For open heart surgery
   d. For baldness treatments

10. Who won the 1980 U. S. presidential election?
    a. Carter
    b. Nixon
    c. Eisenhower
    d. Reagan

11. How many days were the Americans held hostage in Iran?
    a. 245
    b. 365
    c. 444
    d. 502

Constructed Response

12. Explain why Khomeini had more power among the people than the shah. Use details from the selection to support your answer.

_____
_____
_____
_____
_____
_____

Saddam Hussein and Desert Storm

Fireworks in the Middle East

In 1991, Americans sat glued to their television sets as they watched an amazing display of fireworks in the Middle East. The world's attention focused on Saddam Hussein, the ruler of Iraq. He vowed that if the United States tried to stop him, he would create the "mother of battles." Hussein's record was one of plots and intrigues, murders, betrayals, and self-glorification. His name, Saddam, means "one who confronts." He had confronted the Iranians in a war that had killed thousands on both sides. He had confronted the Kurds, who wanted independence, and killed thousands of them with chemical weapons. With the fourth-largest army in the world (a million men in uniform), he confidently predicted that Iraq could beat any combination of countries that might oppose him.

Iraqi President Saddam Hussein

Despite his "bad guy" image in the rest of the world, Iraqis saw Hussein as a bold leader who took care of his people. In the slums of the Middle East, he was the one who stood up against the Western **imperialists**. His oil money went not only into the military, but into food and education programs; Iraq's literacy rate was the highest in the region. He was popular, but feared. His secret police punished any who opposed him. He shot opponents and required cabinet members to execute traitors, as well.

Bergan Oil Field Set on Fire During the Iraqi Invasion of Kuwait, January 1991

Iraq Invades Kuwait

In July 1990, Hussein started threatening Kuwait, Iraq's small neighbor to the south and east. He had long resented the wealth of Kuwait and the rich lifestyle of its people. With a small population and **prosperity**, Kuwaitis lived in ease, with the government providing everything from education through college to free drinking water for its people. He charged that Kuwait (1) was really a province of Iraq, (2) was illegally stealing oil from the Iraqi Rumaili oil field, (3) had over-produced oil beyond its OPEC limits, and (4) had lent millions to Iraq during the **Iraq-Iran conflict** and had the nerve to want it paid back. Hussein said Kuwait's systematic, deliberate, and contemptuous actions amounted to military aggression.

On August 1, 1990, Iraq invaded Kuwait, and many Kuwaitis, including the royal family, fled the country. Those remaining behind suffered brutal treatment at the hands of the Iraqis. The United States demanded Iraq's withdrawal. An Iraqi diplomat predicted that the United States and Iraq would go to war, and "America will lose and America will be humiliated."

President Bush Builds a Coalition of Nations

British Prime Minister Margaret Thatcher advised President George H.W. Bush to build a **coalition** of nations to force Iraq out. By the time war began, 28 nations had sent 698,000 troops. Even Egypt and Syria sent troops. West Germany and Japan sent no troops, but they gave much needed financial support to the coalition. Russia cooperated by stopping arms shipments to Iraq and tried to persuade Iraq to withdraw. Saddam Hussein stubbornly refused.

Leading coalition forces was U.S. General Norman Schwarzkopf, who had support from General Colin Powell (chairman of the U.S. Joint Chiefs of Staff) and U.S. Secretary of Defense Dick Cheney, in assembling the operation. The weapons facing Iraq included the new Tomahawk missiles and the older Patriot missiles (able to blow up Scud missiles in the air). Ground forces were supported by the Abrams tanks. A variety of aircraft were used: **stealth bombers** (not visible on radar screens), B-52s, F-11s, Apache helicopters, and others. Naval power included the U.S.S. *Missouri* to soften Iraqi positions along the coast.

On November 29, 1990, the **United Nations** warned Iraq that it had to be out of Kuwait by January 15, 1991, and return all American and British hostages it held. Talks by the United States and Russia with Iraq were futile. On January 13, Iraq made it clear that it had no intention of giving in. Hussein warned this would be the "mother of all wars" and thousands of Americans would die.

U.S. Navy F-14A Tomcat flies over burning Kuwaiti oil well during Operation Desert Storm.

Coalition Forces Attack Iraq

The U.S. military operation against Iraq was called **Operation Desert Storm**. On January 16, air attacks on Iraq began, and within days, most of the Iraqi air force was destroyed. To save his best 142 planes, Hussein sent them to neutral Iran, which did not return them until after the war was over. Baghdad and other Iraqi cities were defenseless against the air attacks, since their radar installations had been the first targets of the stealth bombers. Some effort was made by Russia to convince Hussein to quit, but he refused to give a date for withdrawal from Kuwait.

Saddam Hussein hoped that if he could provoke Israel to attack Iraq, Arab members of the coalition might withdraw. Scuds were aimed at Tel Aviv, and some hit in the city, but the United States persuaded Israel not to strike back. Patriot missile teams were sent to Israel. The only Arab country giving Iraq any real support was Jordan.

A field artillery unit from the Arkansas Army National Guard heads into battle during Operation Desert Storm.

The ground war broke out Sunday, February 24; the "mother of all battles" was over in 100 hours. Morale of Iraqi troops broke quickly, and large units raised the white flag of surrender. With Kuwait about to be lost, Iraqis set fire to oil rigs, creating a blanket of thick smoke over the country. Kuwait City was recaptured February 27, and a conditional cease-fire was signed the next day. Iraq agreed to give up any claim to Kuwait, surrender its prisoners, and return all stolen property.

Desert Storm Ends

The war, now known as the **Persian Gulf War**, ended on February 28, 1991, with Hussein still in power. Within a few weeks, he was his old, defiant self, refusing to let the United Nations into factories believed to be capable of producing chemical and atomic weapons. U.N. resolutions and economic **sanctions** seemed only to make Hussein more defiant.

Egypt and the Middle East — Saddam Hussein and Desert Storm

Name: _____   Date: _____

Knowledge Check

Matching

_____ 1. prosperity
_____ 2. coalition
_____ 3. Desert Storm
_____ 4. sanction
_____ 5. stealth bomber
_____ 6. United Nations
_____ 7. Persian Gulf War

a. a penalty given to a country for disobeying a law or rule
b. U. S. military aircraft that is difficult to detect by radar
c. the condition of being successful or wealthy
d. name of the conflict between Iraq and a coalition of the U.S. and its allies from August 2, 1990, to February 28, 1991
e. a group of nations that agree to work together
f. name of the U.S. military operation against Iraq in 1991
g. an organization founded to preserve world peace and settle disputes

Multiple Choice

8. What does Saddam mean in Arabic?
   a. "Mother of battles"
   b. "One who eats alone"
   c. "One who confronts"
   d. "Bad guy"

9. Who commanded the coalition forces?
   a. Norman Schwarzkopf
   b. Dick Cheney
   c. Colin Powell
   d. Ronald Reagan

10. How long did the "mother of all battles" last?
    a. 1,000 hours
    b. 10 hours
    c. 100 hours
    d. 300 hours

Constructed Response

11. Explain why Iraq invaded Kuwait. Use at least two details from the selection to support your answer.

_____
_____
_____
_____
_____
_____
_____

The PLO and Israel

Yasser Arafat

Yasser Arafat

Yasser Arafat became the leader of **al-Fatah** (a group determined to drive the Israelis from Palestine) in 1964. An Egyptian by birth, Arafat was trained as an engineer and as a demolition expert by Egypt's army. In 1969, he became the leader of the **Palestine Liberation Organization (PLO)**. This group wanted to unite Palestinian Arabs who had been moved out of their homeland by the creation of the nation of Israel. They wanted an independent state of Palestine to be formed.

Israel Faces Many Problems

Surrounded by Arabs and with Arabs living in their land, Israel's Jews faced serious problems, especially after the Yom Kippur War of 1973. By seizing the **West Bank**, they added one million Arabs to their population.

Israel gave the people of the West Bank the right to hold elections. The men elected were more **radical** than the Israelis wanted; instead of calming the Palestinians down, stone-throwing and **terrorist** incidents occurred. The PLO blamed trigger-happy Israeli soldiers. The Israelis blamed troublemakers stirred up by Israel's enemies: Iraq, Syria, and Egypt.

In 1977, President Anwar Sadat of Egypt went to Israel and offered peace in return for Israel giving up the Sinai Desert, taken in 1967. The final treaty was signed in 1979. Israel was to pull back from the Sinai in three stages, and trade and diplomatic relations would begin the next year.

Egypt and Israel were happy, but the Palestinians were not. They felt that Sadat had ignored their needs completely. PLO raids out of Lebanon increased. Israel's air force bombed Palestinian bases in Lebanon.

Young Palestinians were fed up with the PLO. They saw the Israelis as colonial rulers who denied them a homeland and jobs. They struck back at the Israeli army that shot and tear-gassed them. However, their special anger was directed toward Israelis building settlements on the West Bank. They called their movement the **Intifada**, or "shaking off." Beginning in 1987, settlers and Intifada fighters traded terrorist acts against each other and created a political crisis for Israel. Israel's two major political parties disagreed

Egyptian President Anwar Sadat (left) spoke to the Israeli Knesset in Jerusalem in November 1977.

on how to handle the situation. Israel's public was about evenly divided on the issue. This Intifada gradually came to an end after 1991 when a new round of peace talks began.

A second Intifada broke out from 2000 to 2004 with fighting between Palestinians and Israelis. It is estimated that over 3,200 Palestinians and 950 Israelis were killed in that time period. Violence decreased after 2004, but periodic attacks still occur.

Attempts at Peace

Arafat was in trouble. He had backed Iraq in the Gulf War. He could no longer expect financial support from Russia, and he had angered the Saudis and the other Arab states that fought Iraq. Inside the PLO, a more radical **Hamas** faction had been growing since 1987. Arafat had no choice except to talk with Israel.

In 1991, a Middle East peace conference was held at Madrid. The goal was to start peace **negotiations** that would lead to closer cooperation and reconciliation between the countries of the Middle East. In 1993 at the Oslo Accords, the PLO recognized Israel's right to exist in peace. Israel, in turn, recognized the PLO as the representative of the Palestinian people. The Accords also granted the Palestinians the right to self-government in the Gaza Strip and the city of Jericho in the West Bank. The Palestinian National Authority was created in 1994 as a temporary organization to govern these areas. However, no final negotiations between the PLO and Israel have taken place, so the Palestinian National Authority remains in control of the West Bank. The Hamas government has control over the Gaza Strip.

Israeli Prime Minister Yitzhak Rabin (left) and PLO Chairman Yasser Arafat (right) shake hands in front of President Bill Clinton at the White House September 13, 1993. It was believed to be the first such handshake between Israel and the PLO. The two signed agreements made possible by the Oslo Accords.

Since Arafat's death in 2004, Mahmoud Abbas has been the president of the Palestinian National Authority and the leader of the PLO. Elections are set to be held in the Palestinian territories in May 2012. However, recent uprisings associated with the **Arab Spring** movement of 2011 may delay those elections.

Egypt and the Middle East | The PLO and Israel

Name: _____ Date: _____

Knowledge Check

Matching

____ 1. al-Fatah
____ 2. terrorist
____ 3. Hamas
____ 4. radical
____ 5. Intifada
____ 6. West Bank
____ 7. negotiations

a. a person who uses fear and violence to gain political goals
b. a person who advocates thorough or complete political or social reform
c. area between Israel and Jordan on the west bank of the Jordan River; populated mostly by Palestinians
d. a group determined to drive the Israelis from Palestine
e. an organization founded in 1987 with the aim of establishing an Islamic state in Palestine
f. talks that try to bring about compromise and agreement
g. the Arabic term that translates to "shaking off" and is modernly used as a term of rebellion

Multiple Choice

8. What group did Yasser Arafat head in 1964?
   a. al-Fatah
   b. PLO
   c. Yom Kippur
   d. Hamas

9. Which group in Israel did the Intifada fighters especially dislike?
   a. the Hamas faction
   b. Jewish settlers on the West Bank
   c. the radical leaders
   d. Jewish settlers on the East Bank

10. How did conquering the West Bank add to Israel's problems?
    a. It added 1 million more Arabs.
    b. It added 2 million more Arabs.
    c. It added 500,000 more Arabs.
    d. It added 3 more million Arabs.

Constructed Response

11. Explain why Egyptian President Anwar Sadat went to Israel in 1977. Use details from the selection to support your answer.

_____

_____

_____

_____

_____

_____

The United States and the Middle East

Since the end of World War II, increased violence has caused many problems for the Middle East and for nations around the world. Many Muslims resent foreign influence in their countries. They want to rid the Middle East of non-Islamic influences. They demand a return to a strict version of Islamic law. Some of the groups are using violence to accomplish these goals. These people have been labeled **terrorists**.

The United States has been a target for terrorism because of its presence in the Middle East. On October 12, 2000, the USS *Cole*, a naval destroyer, sat anchored in a port in Yemen. It was struck by a bomb. This attack killed 17 U.S. sailors. **Al-Qaeda**, an Islamic terrorist group, claimed credit for attacking the ship.

Planes hijacked by terrorists hit the Twin Towers of the World Trade Center on September 11, 2001.

A Day of Terror

On September 11, 2001, Islamic terrorists **hijacked** four jet planes. They flew two planes into the Twin Towers of the World Trade Center in New York City. One jet flew into the Pentagon, near Washington, D.C. The fourth plane crashed in a wooded area in Pennsylvania after passengers tried to take back control of the plane. About 3,000 people died in these attacks. Al-Qaeda claimed responsibility for the attacks. It was believed the members of this terrorist group were hiding in Afghanistan.

Afghan War

In response to the 9/11 terrorist attacks, the United States, under the administration of President George W. Bush, and the United Kingdom joined with the Afghan United Front and launched an attack on Afghanistan. On October 7, 2001, early combat operations signaled the start of **Operation Enduring Freedom**, the official name used by the U.S. government for the war in Afghanistan. The goal was to dismantle the al-Qaeda terrorist organization, remove the **Taliban** regime from power in Afghanistan, and create a democratic state. In 2002, a new government took power in Afghanistan. U.S. troops remained to help maintain the peace. In 2011, **Osama bin Laden**, the founder of al-Qaeda and the mastermind behind the 9/11 terrorist attack, was killed by a team of United States **Special Forces**, including Navy SEALs and Central Intelligence Agency (CIA) operatives. In 2011, President Barack Obama started withdrawing troops from Afghanistan and pledged to turn over the nation's security to the Afghan people by 2014.

Osama bin Laden was the leader of the terrorist group al-Qaeda.

Iraq War

In January 2003, a coalition led by the United States invaded Iraq. President Bush was advised that Iraq might have weapons of mass destruction. The invasion was initiated when Iraqi President Saddam Hussein refused to cooperate with weapons inspectors sent by the United Nations. In 2004, the United States transferred sovereignty of Iraq to a new government. After being captured, Saddam Hussein was tried in an Iraqi court of law. He was found guilty and executed. In 2011, President Obama announced that U.S. forces would leave Iraq by the end of the year, bringing the U.S. mission in Iraq to an end.

Egypt and the Middle East / The United States and the Middle East

Name: _____ Date: _____

Knowledge Check

Matching

___ 1. hijack
___ 2. al-Qaeda
___ 3. Taliban
___ 4. Special Forces
___ 5. USS *Cole*
___ 6. Operation Enduring Freedom
___ 7. Osama bin Laden

a. a United States naval destroyer
b. the official name used by the U.S. government for the war in Afghanistan
c. units of the U.S. military specially trained in guerrilla warfare, such as the Navy SEALs or Army Rangers
d. the founder of al-Qaeda
e. the extreme Islamist group who controlled the government of Afghanistan
f. an Islamic terrorist organization founded by Osama bin Laden in 1988
g. to take over the operation of an airplane by force

Multiple Choice

8. What year did a new government take power in Afghanistan after the Taliban was removed?
   a. 2001
   b. 2003
   c. 2002
   d. 2004

9. Who was the President of the United States during the 9/11 terrorist attacks?
   a. Barack Obama
   b. George W. Bush
   c. Jimmy Carter
   d. Bill Clinton

10. Who was tried and executed by an Iraqi court?
    a. Osama bin Laden
    b. Yasser Arafat
    c. Mohamed Atta
    d. Saddam Hussein

U.S. Navy SEALs in a Training Exercise

Constructed Response

11. Explain why a United States-led coalition invaded Iraq in January 2003. Use details from the selection to support your answer.

_____
_____
_____
_____
_____

Arab Spring

In late 2010 and early 2011, a **democratic** uprising started in the Arab country of Tunisia and then rapidly spread across the Middle East. This time of pro-democracy **rebellion** is known as the **Arab Spring**. It is also called the Arab Awakening, since the movement has lasted much longer than the spring season. Social networking through the Internet and cell phones played an important role in mobilizing the rebellion in each country.

TUNISIA: The Tunisian Revolution began in December 2010. In 2011, a new Islamic government formed, promising to bring **reform** and a Western-style democracy to Tunisia.

Rebellion Spreads

Protestors in Cairo, Egypt's, Tahrir Square, were supported by the military.

EGYPT: In January of 2011, **protests** began in Cairo, Egypt, and spread throughout the country. The major demonstrations were held in Tahrir Square in Cairo. In February, Hosni Mubarak **resigned** his presidency and handed power to the army. In March, the interim military government held elections. Mubarak is currently on trial for crimes against the people of Egypt.

LIBYA: The uprising in Libya became violent when government forces under the leadership of Muammar Qaddafi used military force against the protesters. NATO led aerial bomb strikes on the Libyan military in an effort to stop the attacks. In October of 2011, Qaddafi was killed by rebel fighters. Rebel leaders formed an **interim** government.

JORDAN: In January of 2011, protests began in Jordan. The protesters did not want to oust King Abdullah. The main goals of the protests were to lower food prices and have free and fair elections. King Abdullah II met with different groups and listened to their demands. In October, he promised to reform the government. He dissolved the parliament and removed the prime minister.

BAHRAIN: Protests for democracy erupted in Bahrain in February of 2011. The rebellion began online. The protesters wanted more political freedom. Troops from Saudi Arabia intervened. Five different groups formed a **coalition** demanding a transition to a **constitutional monarchy**.

SAUDI ARABIA: King Abdullah had started a series of reforms in an effort to stop the spread of protests before it got to Saudi Arabia. Although there were protests, they were small in comparison to the large groups of people the demonstrations had attracted in other Middle Eastern countries.

SYRIA: Protests in Syria began in January of 2011. The protesters were demanding freedom, human rights, and the end to the emergency law that banned political parties that opposed President Bashar al-Assad. The Syrian government cracked down on the protesters, killing several thousand according to the United Nations. To put an end to the violence, Bashar al-Assad dissolved the government. However, protests and violence continued.

Libyan Rebel Fighters

Egypt and the Middle East

Arab Spring

Name: _____ Date: _____

Knowledge Check

Matching

___ 1. democratic
___ 2. reform
___ 3. Arab Spring
___ 4. resign
___ 5. interim
___ 6. coalition
___ 7. rebellion
___ 8. protest

a. a statement or action that expresses disapproval of something
b. an interval of time between one event
c. a time of pro-democracy rebellion that spread across the Middle East in 2011
d. of or for the people
e. to voluntarily leave a job or other position
f. to make changes in something in order to improve it
g. an act of violent or open resistance to an established government or ruler
h. an alliance with other nations

Multiple Choice

9. When did the Tunisian Revolution begin?
   a. December 2010
   b. December 2011
   c. January 2011
   d. February 2011

10. Who resigned as president of Egypt and was put on trial for crimes against the people?
    a. Muammar Qaddafi
    b. Hosni Mubarak
    c. King Abdullah
    d. Bashar al-Assad

11. What Libyan leader was killed by rebel fighters?
    a. Muammar Qaddafi
    b. Hosni Mubarak
    c. King Abdullah
    d. Bashar al-Assad

Critical Thinking

12. Why were the Internet and cell phones important to the uprisings in the Middle East? Explain your answer.

_____
_____
_____
_____
_____
_____

Egypt and the Middle East

Arab Spring

Name: _____ Date: _____

Map Follow-Up: Nations of the Middle East

Directions: Using an atlas or a map from the Internet, match the names of the nations listed below with the numbers on the map.

___ Saudi Arabia ___ United Arab Emirates ___ Iraq ___ Tunisia

___ Lebanon ___ Jordan ___ Libya ___ Israel

___ Bahrain ___ Turkey ___ Kuwait ___ Iran

___ Oman ___ Pakistan ___ Yemen ___ Egypt

___ Syria ___ Afghanistan ___ Qatar

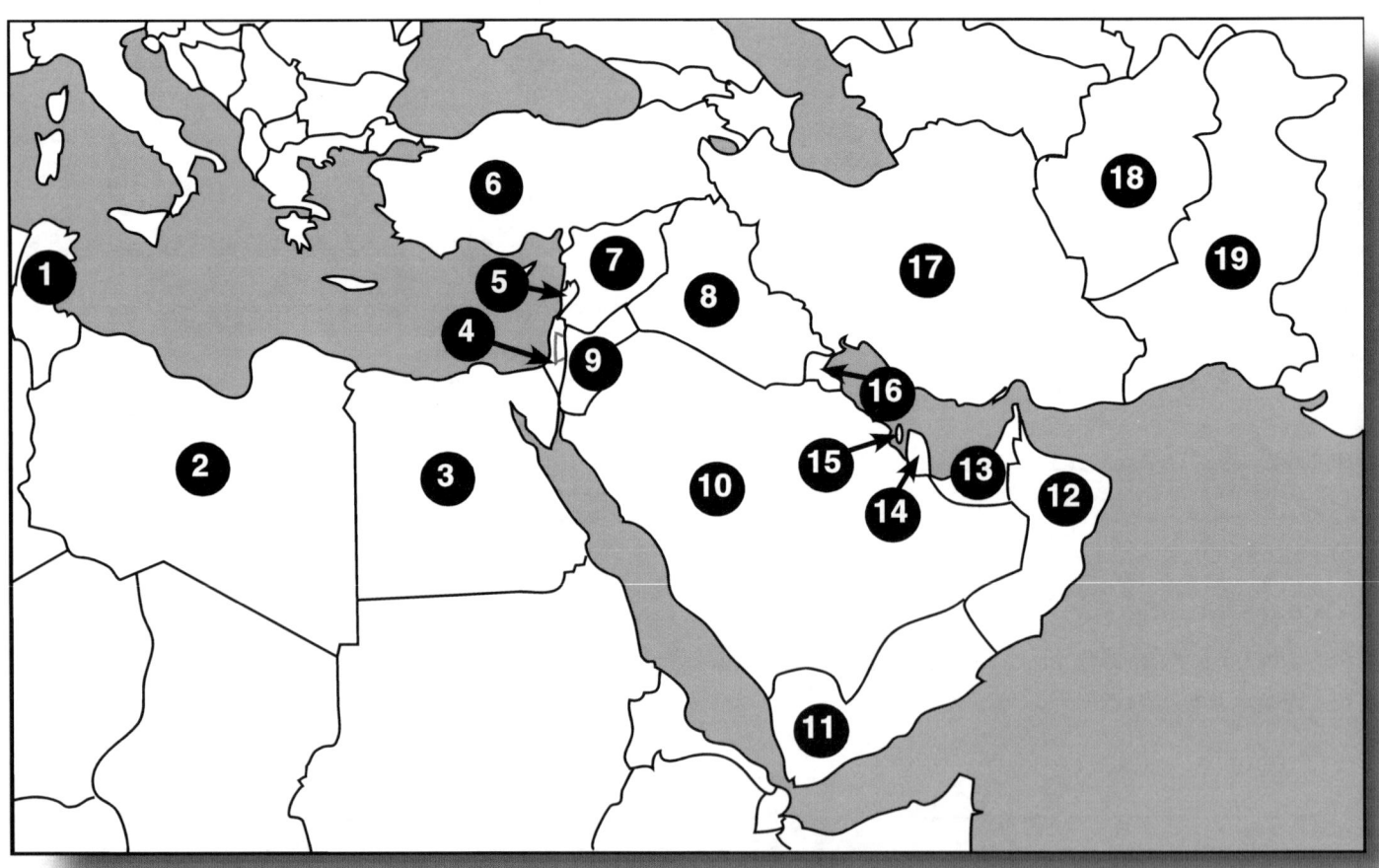

Glossary

Afrika Korps: a German army force sent to North Africa in 1941 under General Rommel
abolished: to put an end to
Abu Simbel: huge temple cut from the rock of a cliff overlooking the Nile; ordered built by Ramses II
afterlife: the life after death
Akhenaton: Pharaoh Amenhotep IV, who changed his name to honor the god Aton
Akhetaton: new city built by Akhenaton on the edge of the desert to honor the god Aton; now called Amarna
al-Fatah: a group determined to drive the Israelis from Palestine
alphabet: a system of writing with characters that stand for sounds
al-Qaeda: a Muslim terrorist organization founded by Osama bin Laden in 1988
alliance: an agreement between countries to work together in war or trade
Amarna period: an era of Egyptian history during the latter half of the Eighteenth Dynasty; from the modern name of the city Akhenaton founded on the edge of the desert
ambassador: a person who is sent by a country as its official representative to a foreign country
Amon-Re: the king of the Egyptian gods; the sun god
amulet: an ornament or small piece of jewelry thought to give protection against evil, danger, or disease
anarchy: a state of disorder due to the absence of authority
Anatolia: ancient name for part of modern-day Turkey
Anubis: the judge of the dead in Egyptian mythology; had the head of a jackal
Arabian-American Oil Company: a petroleum partnership between U.S. firms and Saudi Arabia, 1933–1990
Arab Bureau: a group of Arabs organized by T.E. Lawrence during World War I to help drive the Turks from Arab soil
Arab Spring: time of pro-democracy rebellion in the Middle East that started in late 2010 and early 2011; also called Arab Awakening
archaeologist: a person who studies the remains of past cultures
armistice: an agreement to stop fighting
arms: weapons
assassinate: to murder by sudden or secret attack as for political reasons
Aswan Dam: dam built on the Nile River to increase Egypt's electrical output and control flooding
Aton: the solar disc god of Egyptian mythology; worshipped by the pharaoh Akhenaton

ayatollah: a Shiite religious teacher in Iran
Balfour Declaration: a statement issued by the British government favoring setting up a national home for Jews in Palestine
barbarians: uncivilized tribes from the north of the Roman Empire
barrel: a container holding fifty-five gallons of oil
Ba'ath: the largest Syrian political party
battering ram: a large, heavy wooden beam used to beat down the wall or gate of a city being attacked
benevolent: to organize for the purpose of doing good
bent pyramid: a pyramid whose base is steeper than its top half
Bes: one of the Egyptian gods of the family
Bible: the sacred text of Christians
Bosporus: narrow strait of water that connects the Mediterranean Sea and the Black Sea
Byzantine civilization: civilization that combined elements of Roman, Hellenistic, and Middle Eastern culture
Byzantine Empire: the Eastern Roman Empire; also known as Byzantium
caliph: a Muslim leader who had both political and religious authority
calligraphy: the Arabic handwriting designed in an artistic style
campaign: a series of military operations
capital punishment: death by execution for committing a crime
cease-fire: a temporary suspension of fighting
ceremonial: the system of rules to be observed at a formal or religious occasion
chariot: a light, two-wheeled horse-drawn vehicle used in ancient warfare and racing
Christianity: a religion founded in Judea about 2,000 years ago based on the life and teachings of Jesus Christ
Christians: the followers of Jesus and his teachings
civilization: a culture that has developed systems of specialization, religion, learning, and government
city-state: unit of government based around a city
coalition: an alliance, especially a temporary one, of people, factions, parties, or nations
colonial: a native or inhabitant of a colony
commerce: the exchange or buying and selling of commodities on a large scale
concentration camps: prison camps where Jews and others were taken to be killed or held prisoner by the Nazis during World War II
conquer: to defeat by force
conquest: the act of conquering
conservative: interested in maintaining existing views, conditions, or institutions; traditional

constitutional monarchy: a form of government in which a monarch acts as head of state following rules of a constitution

Coptic: language that developed as a result of contacts between Egypt and Greece

coup: a rebellion inside a government

count: a European nobleman

covenant: a special agreement

Crimean War: a war from 1853 to 1856 fought over the possession of Ottoman territories around the Black Sea

crucifixion: an execution on a cross

Crusader: a person who went on any of the military expeditions known as the Crusades

Crusades: any of the military expeditions undertaken by European Christians in the 11th, 12th, and 13th centuries to recover the Holy Land from the Muslims

Crusader states: the Christian states in the Middle East during the time of the Crusades

cultural: the ideas, customs, and social behavior of a society

cuneiform: a system of writing used by the Babylonians that used wedge-shaped symbols to represent sounds, ideas, and objects

czars: the kings or emperors of Russia

decipher: to read or interpret

deity: a god or goddess

delta: the flat, fan-shaped land made of silt deposited at the mouth of a river

democratic: of or for the people

depression: a low, sunken hole

devshirme: a tax where people sent young boys to the sultan as slaves

Diaspora: the scattering of Jews to many parts of the world

diplomatic: using negotiations to conduct international relations instead of attacking

dismantled: to take apart or tear down

divine: to be like a god

dynasty: a succession of rulers from one family

earthworks: high banks or other constructions made of earth to serve as defenses against an enemy

Eastern Empire: the eastern part of the Roman Empire after it was divided into two parts

embargo: a restriction that a government puts on the buying and selling of certain goods

embassy: the official residence of an ambassador

emir: an Arab prince

empire: the territory under the authority of a single ruler

epic: to extend beyond the usual or ordinary, especially in size or scope

era: a certain time period in history

eternal: to exist forever

ethics: a set of moral ideas that rule a group's behavior

ethnarch: the ruler of a province or a people

exile: an enforced removal from one's native country

expansion: the action of becoming larger or more extensive

expel: to force someone out of a place or country

fanatics: those who are intensely devoted to a cause

ferried: to be taken across a body of water by boat

feudal: system where nobles held land from the king in return for promises of troops and chariots in time of war

First Intermediate Period: period of anarchy in Egyptian history between the end of the Old Kingdom and the beginning of the Middle Kingdom (ca. 2160–2040 B.C.)

Four Colonels: the group that overthrew Nuri in 1941 and made Rashid Ali the premier of Iraq

Fourteen Points: the formulation of a peace program, presented at the end of World War I by U.S. President Woodrow Wilson

frankincense: a fragrant gum resin obtained from an African tree and burned as incense

geometric: using figures from geometry such as lines, circles, and shapes

god-king: a human ruler believed to be a god or to possess godlike powers or qualities

Golan Heights: a range of hills on the border between Syria and Israel, northeast of the Sea of Galilee

Gospels: the first four books of the New Testament of the Bible; they tell of the life of Jesus

grave robbers: those who steal treasure or bodies from graves, especially the tombs of ancient kings

Great Pyramid: the largest pyramid at Gizeh; built for Khufu

grotesque: a very ugly or distorted figure, creature, or image

guerilla warfare: irregular attacks by small units harrassing and sabotaging the enemy

Haganah: the Jewish underground army in Palestine

Hajj: the Muslim pilgrimage to Mecca that takes place in the last month of the year, expected once of all Muslims (the fifth pillar of Islam)

Hamas: an organization founded in 1987 with the aim of establishing an Islamic state in Palestine

Hatshepsut: the sister and wife of a pharaoh who ruled as pharaoh for 20 years in the place of her stepson, Thutmose III

Hebrews: the members or descendants of a Semitic people claiming descent from Abraham, Isaac, and Jacob; an Israelite; a Jew

Hellenistic: based on the Greek culture spread by the conquest of Alexander the Great

hereditary: a title conferred by or based on inheritance

heresies: controversial opinions or groups, especially ones not accepted by the Roman Catholic Church

hieratic: a cursive form of ancient Egyptian writing; simpler than hieroglyphics

hieroglyphics: the ancient Egyptian system of writing that used symbols to stand for objects, ideas, or sounds
hijack: to take over the operation of an airplane by force
historian: writer, student, or scholar of history
Holy City: the city of Jerusalem that is holy to Jews, Christians, and Muslims
homogeneous: to consist of parts all of the same kind
Hor-pa-khered: Egyptian god who had special power to cure poisonous bites and stings
Horus: an Egyptian god portrayed as a falcon
humane law code: a set of laws based on restitution
humanity: the human race; caring about all people in a group or culture
Hyksos: invaders from Syria and Palestine who defeated the Egyptians with new weapons and horse-drawn chariots
idiomatic: sayings peculiar to or characteristic of a given language
Imhotep: builder of the first Egyptian pyramid; considered a god of wisdom
imperialism: a policy of extending a country's power and influence through diplomacy or military force
imperialists: the people who support or practice imperialism
imported: brought into a country from somewhere else
inaugurated: having gone through a formal ceremony to mark the beginning of a leader's term of office
infantry: a soldier trained and equipped to fight on foot
infidels: the name Christians called all Muslims
inherited: to come into possession of (money, property, or a title) as an heir at the death of the previous holder
inscriptions: the wording on a monument or in a book
interim: an interval of time between one event
Intermediate Period: years during which the central government broke down in between the kingdoms of ancient Egypt
Intifada: the Arabic term that translates to "shaking off"; modernly used as a term of rebellion
invaders: a group of people who enters by force in order to conquer
Iraq-Iran conflict: an armed conflict between the armed forces of Iraq and Iran, lasting from September 1980 to August 1988, making it the longest conventional war of the twentieth century
Iraq War: (2003–2011) invasion of Iraq by a coalition of the United States and its allies that led to the transfer of power from Saddam Hussein to a newly elected Iraqi government
Irgun: a Zionist terrorist organization
Islam: the religion of Muslims based on the teachings of the prophet Muhammad
Islamic: of or about the religion of Muslims based on the teachings of the prophet Muhammad
Islamic Republic Party: a political party in Iran, formed in mid-1979 to assist the Iranian Revolution
Janissaries: the specially trained warrior-slaves of the Ottoman Empire
Jerusalem: the city holy to Jews, Christians, and Muslims
Jesus: a teacher and prophet; his life and sermons formed the basis for Christianity
Jew: a member of the community whose traditional religion is Judaism
Jewish: relating to or characteristic of the Jews
Jews: a group of people whose religion is Judaism
jihad: a holy war undertaken as a sacred duty by Muslims
ka: the term the Egyptians used for the soul
Ka'ba: a sacred Muslim shrine in Mecca
Kaiser: the German king
Knesset: the legislature of Israel
knight: a medieval warrior riding horses and wearing armor
Koran: the sacred text of Islam
Kurd: a member of a tribe of Islamic people living in Kurdistan (parts of Iraq, Iran, and Turkey)
Kuwait Petroleum Corporation: the Kuwaiti national oil company, headquartered in Kuwait City
League of Nations: an international organization created in 1919 by the Allied Powers to try to prevent future wars
legacy: a thing handed down by an ancestor or predecessor
Lehi: a Zionist terrorist group also called the Stern Group
Lower Egypt: the delta region in the north of Egypt
ma'at: the ruling principle of the pharaoh meaning order, justice, and truth
mandate: the authority to control the Middle Eastern countries after World War I
Mapai: the Israel Labor Party
mastabas: the flat tombs for the pharoah's officials
Messiah: a special leader the Jewish people believe will be sent by God to guide them and set up God's rule on Earth. Christians believe Jesus is the Messiah.
metallurgy: the branch of science that deals with the properties of metals
Middle East: a region of southwestern Asia and Northern Africa that stretches from Tunisia to Afghanistan
Middle Kingdom: era in Egypt from 2040–1633 B.C.
modernization: to adopt modern ways
Mongols: the members of any of the traditionally nomadic people of Mongolia
monotheism: a belief in one god
monotheist: a person who worships only one god
monsoon rain: a seasonal wind that brings dry weather in the winter and heavy rains in the summer
monumental: to be great in importance, extent, or size

monument: a statue, building, or other structure erected to commemorate a famous or notable person or event
mortuary temple: a place set aside for the worship of a deceased pharaoh
mosque: a Muslim place of worship
Muhammad: an Arab prophet and founder of Islam
Mujahedin: a military force of Muslim guerilla warriors engaged in a jihad
mummy: the dead body of a human or animal that has been embalmed and prepared for burial in the manner of the ancient Egyptians
Muslim: a follower of the religion of Islam
myrrh: a yellowish-brown to reddish-brown aromatic gum resin obtained from certain trees used in burial of the dead
mythology: a traditional story accepted as history; serves to explain the world view of a people
nationalism: the belief that a particular group of people sharing the same language and culture should form an independent state
navigation: getting a ship or aircraft from place to place
navigator: a person who gets ships and aircraft from place to place
negotiations: talks that try to bring about compromise and agreement
neutral: the position of not taking sides in a war or conflict
New Kingdom: era in Egypt from 1558–1085 B.C.
New Testament: the second part of the Bible
Nile River: river that runs from south to north through Egypt; longest river in the world
noblemen: the men distinguished by high birth or rank
nomad: a member of a people who have no permanent residence and wander from place to place to find fresh pasture for their livestock
nomarchs: governors of Egyptian provinces
Nut: Egyptian sky goddess
oil reserves: the supply of oil that can be brought into production from a nation's oil fields
Old Kingdom: era in Egypt from 2686–2160 B.C.
OPEC: Organization of Petroleum Exporting Countries
optimistic: hopefulness and confidence about the future
Ottoman Empire: a former Turkish empire that was founded about 1300 by Osman and reached its greatest territorial extent under Suleiman in the 16th century
Operation Desert Storm: name of the U.S. military operation against Iraq in 1991
Operation Enduring Freedom: the official name used by the U.S. government for the war in Afghanistan beginning in 2001
Osama bin Laden: the founder of the terrorist organization al-Qaeda
pagan: the religious beliefs other than those of the established main world religions

Palestine Liberation Organization: (PLO) a political and military organization formed in 1964 to unite various Palestinian Arab groups and ultimately to bring about an independent state of Palestine
papyrus: a kind of paper made from a reed plant (papyrus) that grows along the Nile; ancient Egyptians used it for writing
paratroops: soldiers trained and equipped to parachute from an airplane
Pax Romana: a period of peace for the Roman Empire that began with the rule of Augustus in about 27 B.C. and lasted around 200 years
Peel Commission: a commission that was sent to Palestine; it recommended that Palestine be divided into one nation for Jews and another for Arabs
persecution: a policy of arresting, injuring, or killing members of a religious or ethnic group
Persian Gulf War: name of the conflict between Iraq and a coalition of the United States and its allies from August 2, 1990, to February 28, 1991
pharaoh: the title used by the rulers of ancient Egypt
Phoenicians: people who lived in the area of modern-day Lebanon; were the first great navigators of the Middle East; developed the first alphabet
pilgrimage: a journey for religious purposes
pogroms: government-approved attacks on Jewish people and property in Russia
political: of or relating to the government or the public affairs of a country
polygamy: the practice of having more than one spouse at one time
premature: before the proper or usual time
priest: a member of the clergy; someone who leads others in worship
priesthood: the office or position of a priest
prime minister: the head of an elected government
progressive: interested in new ideas and opportunities; moving forward
prophet: a person regarded as an inspired teacher of the will of God
prosperity: the condition of being successful or wealthy
protests: a statement or action that expresses disapproval of something
province: a country or region under the control of another government; a district or division of a country
provincial: to come from a province of a country or empire
pyramids: massive structures built of stone, usually having a square base and four triangular sides that slope upward
Pyramid Texts: the instructions to the pharaoh on how to guide his vessel through the underworld to the sun god
quarry: a place from which stone or other materials are or have been extracted

Ra (or Re): most important Egyptian god; the sun god

radical: a person who advocates thorough or complete political or social reform

Ramadan: the ninth month of the Muslim year, strict fasting is observed from sunrise to sunset

ransom: a sum of money or other payment demanded or paid for the release of a prisoner

realistic: the representation of things as they really are

realm: a kingdom

rebellion: an act of violent or open resistance to an established government or ruler

reform: to make changes in something in order to improve it

refugee: a person who has been forced to leave a country in order to escape war, persecution, or natural disaster

reign: the period during which a monarch rules

rejuvenate: to restore

relief: a type of sculpture in which forms and figures are distinguished from a surrounding plane surface

resigned: to voluntarily leave a job or other position

restitution: restoring; making good; giving an equivalent amount for some injury

reunified: to bring a country back together after being divided

rival: a competitor

Rosetta Stone: a black basalt stone found in 1799 that bears an inscription in hieroglyphics, Demotic characters, and Greek that allowed scholars to understand hieroglyphics for the first time

sacred: to be connected with God or dedicated to a religious purpose

Salat: the ritual prayer of Muslims, performed five times daily in a set form (second pillar of Islam)

sanction: a penalty given to a country for disobeying a law or rule

SAVAK: the Iranian secret police

Sawm: the third pillar of Islam is fasting (done mostly during the month of Ramadan)

scribe: a person who kept records and copied letters and official documents

Second Intermediate Period: period in Egyptian history when the Hyksos were in control (ca. 1674–1558 B.C.)

seize: to capture using force

Seljuk Turks: an aggressive tribe from Central Asia

shah: the Persian word for emperor

Shahadah: the first pillar of Islam is an affirmation of faith

sheik: the leader of an Arab village or family

Shiite Muslim: a Muslim of the Shia branch of Islam

Sobek: Egyptian god of the Nile represented by crocodiles

society: a community of people living in a particular region and sharing customs, laws, and organizations

Special Forces: units of the U.S. military specially trained in guerilla warfare, such as the Navy SEALs or Army Rangers

Sphinx: a large stone sculpture with a lion body and a human head

stealth bomber: U. S. military aircraft that is difficult to detect by radar

stepped pyramid: a pyramid whose sides resemble steps

succession: a group of people or things arranged or following in order; a sequence

Suez Canal: a canal in northeastern Egypt connecting the Mediterranean and Red Seas

sultans: the supreme rulers of the Ottoman Empire

syncretism: the tendency to combine contradictory beliefs

synthesize: to create or develop

Taliban: the extreme Islamist group who controlled the government of Afghanistan at the time of the September 11, 2001, attacks on America

Talmud: a book of instructions for the Jewish people

Tanzimat: the name referring to a period of modernizing reforms instituted under the Ottoman Empire

Tawert: the Egyptian goddess of childbirth; her body had parts from a hippopotamus, crocodile, and lioness

temple: a building devoted to the worship of a god or gods

terrace: a leveled platform of earth built into a hillside

terrorist: a person who uses fear and violence to gain political goals

tomb: a large vault, typically underground, used for burying the dead

Torah: the law of God as revealed to Moses and recorded in the first five books of the Hebrew scriptures

Tudeh Party: an Iranian version of the Communist Party

Tutankhamen: crowned pharaoh at ten years old and died at age 19; famous because his tomb was discovered intact in 1922

turmoil: a state of great disturbance, confusion, or uncertainty

United Arab Republic: a former political union established by Egypt and Syria in 1958 and dissolved in 1961

United Nations: an organization founded in 1945 whose members include most of the world's nations. Its goal is to preserve world peace, settle disputes, and aid international cooperation

Upper Egypt: the land in southern Egypt

veneration: to regard with respect

Wailing Wall (West Wall): a remnant of the retaining wall that underlay the second Temple in Jerusalem

welfare state: a country where the government pays for medical care, education, and other services

West Bank: an area between Israel and Jordan on the west bank of the Jordan river; populated largely by Palestinians

White Paper: a 1939 British document; stating that it was not the policy of the British government that Palestine should become a Jewish State; also known as the MacDonald White Paper

wielded: to have and be able to use power or influence

World War I: a war fought from 1914 to 1918; Great Britain, France, Russia, Belgium, Italy, Japan, the United States, and other allies defeated Germany, Austria-Hungary, Turkey, and Bulgaria.

World War II: the war from 1939–45; the Allies (Great Britain, the Soviet Union, and the United States) defeated the Axis powers of Germany, Italy, and Japan; also called the Second World War

Yahweh: a Hebrew name for God

Yom Kippur: Jewish religious observance with fasting and prayer; the Day of Atonement

Young Turks: the members of a Turkish reformist and nationalist political party active in the early 20th century

Zakat: an obligatory payment made annually under Islamic law on certain kinds of property to support the poor (the fourth pillar of Islam)

Zionist: a person in favor of the return of the Jewish people to their homeland and favoring the establishment in Palestine of a national home for the Jews

---

Answer Keys

Time Line for the Middle East (page 5)
Order of Events
A. 10 B. 7 C. 3 D. 9
E. 6   F. 4 G. 5 H. 8
I. 1   J. 2

True or False
1. F 2. T 3. T 4. T
5. F

Constructed Response
6. Answers will vary but could include: A time line provides a visual list of events in order. It lets people easily see when important events took place, in what order they occurred, and the amount of time that passed between them.

The Rise of Ancient Egypt Knowledge Check (page 8)
Matching
1. g 2. d 3. a 4. e
5. c 6. b 7. f

Multiple Choice
8. b 9. a 10. c

Constructed Response
11. The Egyptian civilization was shaped by its close proximity to a river. The Nile served as an avenue for transportation and irrigation. Almost all Egyptians lived in the narrow belt and the fan-shaped delta of fertile land shaped by the Nile.

The Pyramids and the Sphinx Knowledge Check (page 11)
Matching
1. f 2. b 3. d 4. a
5. g 6. h 7. c 8. e

Multiple Choice
9. d 10. b 11. a

Constructed Response
12. They wouldn't like cremation. They believed a complete body was needed to house the soul, or ka, so they developed a process to keep the body preserved.

Map Follow-Up (page 12)
1. Sudan   2. Egypt
3. Nile River
4. Mediterranean Sea
5. Sinai Peninsula 6. Israel
7. Jordan   8. Gulf of Suez
9. Saudi Arabia   10. Red Sea
Teacher check cities.

Explore Egyptian Numerals (page 13)
1. a. 34   b. 266
   c. 11,320   d. 342,156
2.

The Egyptian Gods Knowledge Check (page 15)
Matching
1. d 2. e 3. c 4. g
5. f 6. b 7. a

Multiple Choice
8. a 9. d 10. c

Constructed Response
11. The Egyptians mixed conflicting beliefs. Sometimes Egyptian mythology taught that the sky was a goddess named Nut who stretched over the earth, but at other times they believed it was a gigantic cow. There were over 2,000 gods. The gods took many forms, and sometimes real people were turned into gods, such as Imhotep. These different beliefs were all seen as valid ways of describing nature.

The End of the Old Kingdom Knowledge Check (page 17)
Matching
1. d 2. f 3. c 4. a
5. b 6. g 7. e

Multiple Choice
8. c 9. b 10. d

Constructed Response
11. As the pharaoh's power declined, there was no one to administer justice or manage irrigation. Egypt suffered with drought and famine, tombs were ransacked, and anarchy reigned. They may also have spent too much on building pyramids.

Egypt and the Middle East — Answer Keys

The Middle Kingdom
Knowledge Check (page 19)
Matching
1. g   2. a   3. b   4. f
5. d   6. c   7. e
Multiple Choice
8. d   9. b   10. a
Constructed Response
11. Because papyrus scrolls used for many kinds of writing survived in Egyptian tombs. Some of the scrolls contained prayers, spells, historical records, letters, business contracts, and royal proclamations.

The End of the Middle Kingdom
Knowledge Check (page 22)
Matching
1. d   2. c   3. a   4. b
5. e   6. f
Multiple Choice
7. d   8. a   9. b
Constructed Response
10. They wanted to improve Egyptian life through foreign trade. They weakened the power of the provincial governors. Also, a gigantic irrigation project moved water from the Nile to a natural depression called Lake Faiyum where it could be stored for use during the dry season.

The New Kingdom
Knowledge Check (page 24)
Matching
1. f   2. d   3. a   4. b
5. g   6. e   7. c
Multiple Choice
8. b   9. a   10. c
Constructed Response
11. It was cut from the rock of a cliff overlooking the Nile. The Egyptians removed an estimated 365,000 tons of rock to create the structure. It was designed in such a way that on two mornings each year, 30 days before the spring equinox and 30 days after the autumnal equinox, the sun's rays could penetrate the 200 feet of darkness to light up the statues deep in the temple's interior.

Queen Hatshepsut
Knowledge Check (page 26)
Matching
1. b   2. g   3. e   4. a
5. c   6. d   7. f
Multiple Choice
8. a   9. d   10. a
Critical Thinking
11. Answers will vary.

Akhenaton the Bizarre
Knowledge Check (page 28)
Matching
1. c   2. g   3. d   4. e
5. a   6. b   7. f
Multiple Choice
8. d   9. b   10. a
Constructed Response
11. Some say that he suffered from a glandular disorder that deformed his body. Others say that he wanted to emphasize his closeness with a creator god.

The Tomb of Tutankhamen
Knowledge Check (page 30)
Matching
1. d   2. b   3. c   4. e
5. h   6. a   7. f   8. g
Multiple Choice
9. c   10. a   11. d
Constructed Response
12. The priests of Amon-Re re-established their authority. The worship of Aton was abolished, and Akhenaton's city was abandoned. The temples to Aton were dismantled and the materials shipped across the river to build new temples to Amon-Re.

The Rise and Fall of Empires in the Middle East
Knowledge Check (page 32)
Matching
1. f   2. d   3. g   4. b
5. c   6. e   7. a
Multiple Choice
8. b   9. b   10. b
Constructed Response
11. The old Babylonian law codes required an eye for an eye. The Hittite laws were based on restitution. For example, arsonists were required to replace property they set afire. A murderer could go free after they paid the family of the victim a large amount of silver, slaves, or land.

The Creative Nations of Phoenicia and Israel
Knowledge Check (page 34)
Matching
1. b   2. c   3. d   4. f
5. a   6. e   7. g
Multiple Choice
8. d   9. a   10. b
Constructed Response
11. The Phoenicians invented the alphabet to make trade easier. They also left colonies all over the Mediterranean that turned into important cities. They spread the knowledge of weaving, glassmaking, and metallurgy developed by their neighbors in the Middle East throughout the ancient world.

Alexander the Great Conquers His World
Knowledge Check (page 36)
Matching
1. d   2. e   3. f   4. b
5. c   6. a   7. g
Multiple Choice
8. c   9. a   10. d   11. b
Constructed Response
12. Different cultures could freely mix. There were many great achievements in art, philosophy, and science. The cultural environment also opened up opportunities for new trade between lands very far and different from each other.

The Middle East and the Roman Empire
Knowledge Check (page 38)
Matching
1. f   2. a   3. g   4. b
5. e   6. d   7. c
Multiple Choice
8. b   9. d   10. a

Constructed Response
11. They left Jerusalem and went in many directions: Europe, North Africa, and the Middle East. A major center for Jews was Baghdad. There, Jewish scholars were trained in academics, and study of the Talmud (Jewish law) continued. In Europe, they came under Christian rule.

Christianity Conquers Rome
Knowledge Check (page 40)
Matching
1. f   2. g   3. a   4. d
5. e   6. b   7. c
Multiple Choice
8. c   9. d   10. a
Constructed Response
11. The Roman Empire was in decline. Barbarians began to threaten the borders. Meanwhile, high taxes, plagues, and civil wars disrupted life within the empire. The empire was too big for one man to rule.

From the Sands of Arabia Comes Islam
Knowledge Check (page 42)
Matching
1. d   2. f   3. a   4. e
5. b   6. c   7. g
Multiple Choice
8. a   9. a   10. a
Constructed Response
11. Many leaders and prophets like Abraham and Moses are held in high esteem by Muslims and are found in the Koran. The Muslims also believe in only one God whom they call Allah. The Koran mentions Jesus, but they see him as a prophet like Muhammad.

The Islamic Golden Age
Knowledge Check (page 44)
Matching
1. d   2. f   3. g   4. e
5. a   6. b   7. c
Multiple Choice
8. c   9. d   10. a

Constructed Response
11. The Arabs were great warriors and were led by brilliant generals like Khalid ibn-al-Walid. They believed they were fighting a Jihad. The Byzantine Empire was exhausted by warfare against the other great power of the Middle East, Persia. As a result, all of Persia and all of the Byzantine Empire except Turkey quickly fell to the caliph's warriors.

Crusaders Descend upon the Middle East
Knowledge Check (page 47)
Matching
1. e   2. f   3. g   4. a
5. b   6. h   7. d   8. c
Multiple Choice
9. b   10. d   11. a
Critical Thinking
12. Answers will vary.

The Middle East Under the Power of the Turks
Knowledge Check (page 49)
Matching
1. d   2. e   3. f   4. c
5. a   6. g   7. b
Multiple Choice
8. d   9. c   10. b
Constructed Response
11. They fell behind the Europeans in technology. Religious leaders repressed the use of printing presses so books were rare. Also, corruption had weakened the sultan's ability to rule.

Map Follow-Up (page 50)
True or False
1. T   2. F   3. F   4. T
5. F
Critical Thinking
6. Answers will vary.

New Forces for Change in the Ottoman Empire
Knowledge Check (page 52)
Matching
1. c   2. d   3. f   4. g
5. e   6. a   7. b
Multiple Choice
8. a   9. b   10. b

Constructed Response
11. Napoleon's invasion impressed upon them the superior technological capabilities of a European power. Middle Easterners redoubled their pleas for reform and modernization.

World War I and the Middle East
Knowledge Check (page 55)
Matching
1. f   2. e   3. d   4. c
5. b   6. a   7. g
Multiple Choice
8. a   9. c   10. b
Constructed Response
11. Turkey was eager to get into Europe's war on Germany's side, thinking that with the Kaiser's help they could seize land in the Caucasus region from Russia. In August 1914, they signed a secret alliance with Germany and waited until October to announce it. By getting involved, they were going to cross England, Russia, and France.

The Mandate System
Knowledge Check (page 58)
Matching
1. c   2. a   3. e   4. f
5. d   6. g   7. h   8. b
Multiple Choice
9. b   10. d   11. c
Constructed Response
12. A parliament began, transportation and communications greatly improved, and its oil resources were developed.

The Middle East and World War II
Knowledge Check (page 61)
Matching
1. d   2. f   3. g   4. e
5. a   6. b   7. c
Multiple Choice
8. b   9. a   10. c   11. d
Critical Thinking
12. Answers will vary. Possible answers include its location and the importance of oil.

Israel
Knowledge Check (page 64)
Matching
1. f 2. h 3. b 4. g
5. e 6. a 7. c 8. i
9. d

Multiple Choice
10. a 11. a 12. d

Constructed Response
13. After Egypt and Syria jointly attacked Israel and took some territory, the Israelis regrouped and fought back. They recovered the ground lost, and drove the Egyptians beyond the Suez Canal. Now, Israel held both of its banks.

Oil Brings Changes to the Middle East
Knowledge Check (page 67)
Matching
1. e 2. h 3. b 4. f
5. a 6. g 7. c 8. d

Multiple Choice
9. c 10. b 11. b

Constructed Response
12. He built sewage and water treatment plants, hospitals, and schools. He paved roads and built a strong air force with the latest planes.

Khomeini Takes on the United States
Knowledge Check (page 71)
Matching
1. d 2. g 3. b 4. h
5. c 6. a 7. e 8. f

Multiple Choice
9. b 10. d 11. c

Constructed Response
12. He sent taped messages into Iran that were broadcast to the country by religious backers. In October 1978, Khomeini called for a general strike and that was followed the next month by strikes of oil field workers. The success of these efforts paralyzed the economy and made clear that he had more power than the shah. The people were fed up with the shah spending money on arms and being influenced by the United States.

Saddam Hussein and Desert Storm
Knowledge Check (page 74)
Matching
1. c 2. e 3. f 4. a
5. b 6. g 7. d

Multiple Choice
8. c 9. a 10. c

Constructed Response
11. Hussein resented the wealth of Kuwait and the rich lifestyle of its people. He charged that Kuwait (1) was really a province of Iraq, (2) was illegally stealing oil from the Iraqi Rumaili oil field, (3) had overproduced oil beyond its OPEC limits, and (4) had lent millions to Iraq during the Iraq-Iran conflict and had the nerve to want it paid back.

The PLO and Israel
Knowledge Check (page 77)
Matching
1. d 2. a 3. e 4. b
5. g 6. c 7. f

Multiple Choice
8. a 9. b 10. a

Constructed Response
11. He went to Israel to offer peace in return for Israel giving up the Sinai desert taken in 1967. The final treaty was signed in 1979. Israel was to pull back from Sinai in three stages, and trade and diplomatic relations would begin the next year.

The United States and the Middle East
Knowledge Check (page 79)
Matching
1. g 2. f 3. e 4. c
5. a 6. b 7. d

Multiple Choice
8. c 9. b 10. d

Constructed Response
11. It was feared that Iraq had weapons of mass destruction. The invasion was initiated when Iraqi President, Saddam Hussein refused to cooperate with the weapons inspectors sent by the United Nation.

Arab Spring
Knowledge Check (page 81)
Matching
1. d 2. f 3. c 4. e
5. b 6. h 7. g 8. a

Multiple Choice
9. a 10. b 11. a

Critical Thinking
12. Answers will vary. Possible answers include: The protestors were able to use social networking to let people know where and when protests would be held. They could also let the rest of the world know what was happening when the governments shut down the traditional media outlets.

Map Follow-Up (page 82)
1. Tunisia 2. Libya
3. Egypt 4. Israel
5. Lebanon 6. Turkey
7. Syria 8. Iraq
9. Jordan 10. Saudi Arabia
11. Yemen 12. Oman
13. United Arab Emirates
14. Qatar 15. Bahrain
16. Kuwait 17. Iran
18. Afghanistan 19. Pakistan

Bibliography

Many books have been written about all aspects of the history of the Middle East. The bibliography here lists a small sample of books that will help the teacher and the students understand Middle Eastern history.

Adams, Simon. *World War I*. DK Children. 2007.

Adams, Simon. *World War II*. DK Children. 2007.

Ambrose, Stephen. *The Good Fight: How World War II Was Won*. Atheneum Books for Young Readers. 2001.

Bator, Robert. *Daily Life in Ancient and Modern Istanbul*. Runestone Press. 2000.

Charling, Douglas. *Judaism*. DK Children. 2003.

Demi. *Jesus*. Margaret K. McElderry Books. 2005.

Demi. *Muhammad*. Margaret K. McElderry Books. 2003.

Greenblatt, Miriam. *Suleyman the Magnificent and the Ottoman Empire*. Marshall Cavendish Children's Books. 2002.

Hart, George. *Ancient Egypt*. DK Children. 2008.

Miller, Mara. *The Iraq War: A Controversial War in Perspective*. Enslow Publishers. 2010.

Parsons, Jayne. *Crusades*. DK Children. 2001.

Peterson, J. E. *Tensions in the Gulf, 1978-1991 (Making of the Middle East)*. Mason Crest Publishers. 2007.

Price-Hossell, Karen. *The Persian Gulf War*. Heinemann Library. 2003.

Putnam, James. *Eyewitness Pyramid*. DK Publishing. 2011.

Santella, Andrew. *The Persian Gulf War*. Compass Point Books. 2004.

Saunders, Nicholas. *The Life of Alexander the Great*. Brighter Child. 2006.

Sherman, Josepha. *Your Travel Guide to Ancient Israel*. Lerner Publications. 2004.

Souter, Gerry and Janet Souter. *War in Afghanistan and Iraq: The Daily Life of the Men and Women Serving in Afghanistan and Iraq*. Carlton Books. 2011.

Spilsbury, Louise. *Iran*. Heinemann-Raintree. 2011.

Stanley, Diane. *Saladin: Noble Prince of Islam*. HarperCollins. 2002.

Steele, Philip. *Middle East*. Kingfisher. 2006.

Stone, Caroline. *Islam*. DK Children. 2005.

Van Vleet, Carmella. *Great Ancient Egypt Projects You Can Build Yourself*. Nomad Press. 2006.

Wilhelm, Doug. *Alexander the Great: Master of the Ancient World (Wicked History)*. Franklin Watts. 2010.

Wilkinson, Philip. *Christianity*. DK Children. 2006.

Williams, Julie. *Islam: Understanding the History, Beliefs, and Culture (Issues in Focus Today)*. Enslow Publishers. 2008.

Wolfman, Marv. *Homeland: The Illustrated History of the State of Israel*. Nachshon Press, LLC. 2007.